Time's Up!

But,

David Ritchie asks

'What brought us to this?'

Reflections on: Referendums, Regulation, Rulers (including Royals), Radio and TV, Rough Justice, Racism, Relief Work, and the Rest

GBP.

GB Publishing Org

www.gbpublishing.co.uk
www.gbpublishing.co.uk/lifestyle

SCAN ME

Contents

Starting point   1

Current Affairs The EU referendum and its aftermath   4
A tale of a barely united kingdom   4
Great days for fearless newspapers   12
The 1975 referendum: a look back...   13
A club to keep clear of ... perhaps   14

Regulation The regulators   16
What do they do? Are they necessary?   16
No competition – but a regulator imposed anyway   17
Some 'protection' for gas and electricity consumers   19
Getting the 'best' from 'communications'   22
Keeping us all on the right lines...   25
Overseeing health and safety in the workplace   30
Taking action, or not, on the environment   32
'Upholding information rights', whatever that means   34
Keeping watch on surveillance cameras   36
You can bet that gambling is regulated – sort of   38
Deciding what is or is not 'competitive'   41
Trying to see that everyone trades 'properly'   43
Working to ensure charities are charitable   45
Overseeing the way we are persuaded to vote   47
'Ensuring the quality' of health and social care services   50
Aiming to 'improve' health services   53
Taking care of our civil airspace   54
Holding the nuclear industry to account   56
'Assuring value' of some defence spending   57
Trying to make sure that supermarkets behave themselves   58
'An appropriate regime' for forensic science services   59
Some of the regulators link up   60
Regulating the regulators   62

Media   63
The BBC: a public service in decline   63
Ipso facto, press regulator fails to impress   74
Controlling standards in advertising   79

Money   83

Can we bank on regulation?   83
Looking after financial services – and "our" money   88
Keeping a careful eye on what is spent   91
Keeping track of what MPs spend   93
Taking some sort of care of some pensions   94

Justice   97

Court out: you might be lucky ... or not   97

Racism, bigotry and hate crime   109

Why can't people tolerate each other?   109

Politics – 1   115

The worldwide leadership conundrum   115
A regulator in all but name...   135

Politics – 2   140

Britain's greatest Prime Minister?   140

Politics – 3   148

Overseas aid and health: why not tackle the pressing problems?   148

Musings   154

What a wacky world ...   154
'Absolute consideration' given to mind-boggling decision   154
Not a very high opinion of civil servants   154
Protocols. What protocols? Who cares?   155
Keep out of the Chinese Presidents' way   155
Some reluctance to fund the Conservative Party   156
An error to be looked into...   156
A tax system not fit for purpose   156
Kind-hearted organisations agree to payment by instalments   157
Probate fees increase gets great response from Ministry   157
A tax return returned by HMRC   157
Proceeding at a great rate – a floor in the system   158
How big is that again?   158
Variations on a theme   158
Accessibility: no loos is the choice   159
Toughening up on identity checks   159
Awards for "nonsense" and "gibberish"   160

Getting the views of the average taxi driver...   160
An interesting way of treating visitors   161
Service with a smile ... and a brilliant excuse   161
Women's rights ... a long-running issue   162
Just how wrong can anyone be?   162

Last words   **163**
And finally...   163

Acknowledgements   **165**

The Author   **168**

See other GBP titles   **169**

Starting point

"When I use a word," said Humpty Dumpty in rather a scornful tone, "it means just what I choose it to mean – neither more nor less."

– Lewis Carroll in Through the Looking Glass

These jottings are not intended as a comprehensive review of life in the late 20th and early 21st century but rather as a series of essays looking at various aspects of the state of the UK and further afield. As far as governance in particular is concerned, the question will be asked as to how "we" could possibly have got to where we are. Beginning with a certain referendum!

The period from 1979 to 2020 in the UK and elsewhere has been one of great upheaval in which despots have thrived; the standard of leadership worldwide – whether by royals (excluding some ceremonial or constitutional ones) or so-called commoners – ranges from mediocre to extremely poor. Democracy has been under threat in many countries. Oppression, torture and censorship are widespread. Words, including antisemitism, are misused. The level of service provided by government departments and local councils has been steadily declining. The civil service has become ever more impenetrable – the French used to claim, with some truth, that their civil service was the most impenetrable, but the UK has now surpassed it. Overseas aid money is grossly misused – and has been for a long time. Ludicrous proposals are given serious consideration (and that applies to more than just the poll tax). The justice system, particularly in England and Wales, is in an appalling state and needs root and branch reform – improvement might be a better word. There are serious problems with polls, pollsters and "fake news". A massive industry has grown up in the field of "regulation" which impinges on all our lives. And so on, and on...

Research for various chapters uncovered some curious facts. One in particular that caught the eye was a finding from the British Social Attitudes Survey of 2017 which revealed that 33% of Conservative party supporters described themselves as racially prejudiced, compared to 18% of Labour supporters – and yet it's Labour that gets most of the flak for being racist, particularly towards Jewish people. Less odd was that 34% of people who voted Leave in the 2016 referendum on the EU considered themselves to be

1

racially prejudiced while just 18% of Remain voters described themselves in this way.

Large sections of this book are devoted to the UK's regulatory bodies, which constitute a multi-billion pound industry that touches numerous areas of our lives but achieves remarkably little for all the time, effort and expenditure. It was a revelation to the author – and maybe it will be to readers too – just how many of these bodies there are, how many people they employ and how much money they spend. Most of them speak highly, often very highly, of their own achievements, but their best work is seen mainly in the production of annual reports.

The UK as a country has become very concerned, and rightly so, with how we deal with household waste but much less concerned with waste of money. From "smart meters" to HS2, many schemes are poorly thought out with vast amounts of money being poured down enormous drains with little benefit to the population at large – or to the environment. And no one is held to account. When Boris Johnson was Mayor of London, well over £60 million was spent, with his blessing, on preparations for a flash new bridge across the Thames, but not a pile will ever be driven and the money is lost forever from the public purse. Folly after folly.

Certain topics, such as climate change, will be left virtually untouched. It's too great an issue to be considered in any detail here. But in a world where a 16-year-old Swedish lass can talk more impressively about the subject in a few minutes than any number of people with the power to change things can say in decades, it's clear that much is badly wrong. It's so sad that we of current and previous generations have made such a mess that fires consume ever more woodland, houses and animals in Australia and California, to name but two areas; entire species are disappearing at an alarming rate; ice is thawing in huge areas of the earth's surface; wind proves ever more devastating; plastic waste is ruining vast areas of the oceans – yet greed, cruelty and apathy prevail.

We've been warned again and again that time is almost up for keeping this wonderful planet habitable and drastic action is needed, but who will step forward to take it? It shouldn't be left to teenagers but too few older people are willing to get involved. Action in the UK is slow, painfully slow, but where are the people with the courage to speed things up? Just to add, however, by way of counter-balance, that back in 2014 the outgoing chief economist of the Institute of Directors forecast that by 2024 "man-made global warming will have been exposed as a myth". He should get on well with one Donald J. Trump.

The NHS would require a book all of its own to catalogue its virtues and failings, the wonderful work that goes on despite appalling mismanagement. We won't discuss PFI schemes whereby lovely new hospitals have been built but NHS Trusts are left saddled for umpteen years with high rents and maintenance costs so that money intended for healthcare gets diverted into the pockets of landlords. They are only doing what successive governments have allowed them to do, so no blame there, obviously.

Nor will we ask why millions of pounds have been misspent to keep "whistleblowers" or departing staff quiet about serious issues: this is a gross misuse of public funds of which the Department of Health has been fully aware but kept saying it was not its concern. And the lawyers who draw up the "gagging" orders or agreements should be struck off for aiding and abetting such misuse of taxpayers' money. But it goes on. It turns out that lawyers, even barristers, have used such orders on members of staff who have been sexually harassed, or worse, which hardly encourages faith in the legal profession. Churches, universities and even schools have also been busy in the field of "non-disclosure agreements". And we learnt from the findings of a survey published in *The Times* in February 2020 that one in six people working in "the arts and cultural sector" has been subject to a gagging order "to control dissenting voices".

Intriguingly, the Houses of Parliament spent more than £2.4 million on 53 "non-disclosure" agreements with staff between 2013 and 2017, though a spokesperson there said the agreements "included confidentiality clauses but did not prevent those who signed them from whistleblowing". No other information was forthcoming but one could be tempted to ask, "What was the point?"

Gagging, sadly, has been widespread in numerous cases of sexual abuse of children. Give the victims money so they won't tell of their appalling treatment while organisations in which people should be able to put their trust can appear to keep their noses clean.

It has become a feature of life in Britain and elsewhere: silence the messenger and ignore the message. Perhaps that will be the fate of these jottings.

Current Affairs
The EU referendum and its aftermath

A tale of a barely united kingdom

Where else to start, but with Thursday 23rd June 2016, the date of the referendum in the UK and Gibraltar which asked people to vote either to remain in or leave the European Union. The government, led by David Cameron – once described by Barack Obama as a lightweight politician, aptly as it turned out – said it believed the UK should remain but was pretty half-hearted in its efforts to maintain the *status quo*.

On one occasion, the then Chancellor, the smug but dim-witted George Osborne, said that if the UK left the EU, house prices could fall by 18%. Now, was that an argument to stay in or drop out? Many people struggling to get onto the housing ladder would be delighted with such a fall in prices. That is just one example of the ambiguity and confusion of the government's approach.

Some time after the referendum, the Treasury said it was concerned that its reputation might have been damaged by some of the statements made. As this esteemed department is almost always wrong in its assessments, it's hardly likely that its reputation would (or could) have been made to sink any lower.

Pollsters kept predicting that the electorate would choose to remain, proving once again (as in the general elections of 2015 and 2017 and even the USA's 2016 presidential election, to give but a few recent examples) what a waste of time and money such polls and pollsters are. They pretend to have a scientific base for their work and in recent times have generally stopped pointing out what they consider the "margins of error" are. When the margins are quoted, they are often in the region of very few per cent when in reality they are likely to be much greater – even up to as much as 10%. As a result they are entirely misleading and, more often than not, plain wrong.

In short, the polls were way off: 72.2% of the electorate voted by 51.9% to 48.1% (17,410,742 votes to 16,141,241) to leave the EU. Nearly 13 million people didn't vote and over 25,000 ballot papers were rejected for various reasons. More than 21% of the total votes cast were by post – 87.6% of the more than 8.5 million papers issued. There has been much concern expressed about the validity of a substantial proportion of postal votes in both general and local elections but little was said about that this time.

4

It would be interesting to know how the leading "Leave" campaigners – including UKIP's Nigel Farage, the maverick and opportunistic Boris Johnson and the hard-to-fathom Michael Gove, all of whom were aided by various newspapers which turned themselves into political pamphlets (as they frequently do at election times) – would have reacted had the vote been as close the other way. One can imagine them claiming it was too close and trenchantly calling for the referendum to be re-run.

If just two people in every hundred who voted to leave had switched to remain, the slim majority would have disappeared. And there were quite a few voters who declared that they had voted to leave because they didn't like Mr Cameron or for other reasons unrelated to the actual subject of the referendum. None of this stopped the leading Leave campaigners and various newspapers from declaring a resounding victory and shouting down all opposition.

"Remainers" were told, in no uncertain terms, to shut up, stop whingeing and accept the result: they'd had their say at the ballot box, the decision had been made and all opposition should cease. That principle doesn't, of course, apply in other areas of political activity: losers in a general election form the opposition and that opposition is vital for good governance. So why, after a referendum and particularly one as close-run as this, should opposition be silenced? That wouldn't make any sense at all.

Voting patterns were not uniform across the UK. Scotland voted to stay in: 1,661,191 to remain and 1,018,322 seeking to leave, a whopping 24% majority on a 67.2% turnout. Northern Ireland also voted to remain in the EU, by the substantial margin of 11.55%: 440,707 voters wanting to remain against 349,442 seeking to leave in a 62.7% turnout.

Wales and England voted to leave: Wales by a margin of 5% (854,572 to 772,347 on a 71.7% turnout); England by nearly 7% (15,188,406 to 13,266,996 on a 73% turnout). But England was certainly not united in its vote with Londoners voting to remain by a margin of nearly 20% (2,263,519 to 1,513,232 on a 69.7% turnout). So the less densely populated regions of England, coupled with one of the smaller countries of the Union, swung the vote in favour of "Leave" and the entire UK had to go along with them.

And let's not forget little Gibraltar, with its population of just under 32,400: this British Overseas Territory voted by 19,322 to 823 to stay in, a margin of over 90% on an 83.5% turnout. Territories closer to the UK, such as the Isle of Man, Jersey and Guernsey, didn't get a vote as they are not actually part of the UK (who knew?) even though they are part of the customs territory of the EU. All a bit muddled in reality, but the arrangements have suited all the parties involved – and would have continued to suit the UK very well for its post-Brexit future, but alas it is not to be.

The vote was lost and that's that. No matter by how small a margin, a victory is a victory, and claims of illegal funding of the Leave campaign were simply swept aside by discrediting the bringers of such uncomfortable details. The matter had not finished at the time of writing this, but the rather ineffectual Electoral Commission was endeavouring to levy a hefty fine after revealing the campaign had spent more than it should have and in ways that it shouldn't have – the limit being set, on virtually no basis at all, by the Electoral Commission. It was also being claimed, again on no evidence at all, that the "overspending" had not affected the result of the referendum. So what is the point of vast sums being spent on electioneering or referendumering if it has no effect? Such conundrums are too great to be considered here.

David Cameron's resignation, after the referendum left him with egg on his face, led to a new leader – and PM – being installed by the Conservatives: one Mrs Theresa May, a lady who had favoured staying in the EU and was now in charge of getting the country out. It was clear from the start that her heart wasn't really in it and then, having said she wouldn't call a general election, she did so and made a pig's ear of it. Her party lost its majority and she was left in an incredibly weak position – but decided to press on. Such is the elixir of power.

Then came the debate about whether parliament should have a say in implementing the decision of the referendum. Loud voices, including Messrs Farage, Johnson and Gove – along with at least two of the national daily newspapers – wanted to ignore parliament. A very odd approach, especially as one reason many people gave for voting to leave the EU was to see the sovereignty of the British parliament restored.

In November 2016, the High Court ruled that the government did not have the power to trigger Article 50 (the mechanism for leaving the EU) without parliamentary approval and a vote by MPs. The case had been triggered by one Gina Miller, who became the figurehead of the legal fight to get parliament to vote on whether the UK could start the process of leaving the EU. The 51-year-old investment manager stressed that she was not trying to block the decision of the referendum but to have it dealt with through the proper channels – an entirely laudable aim, one might think.

Her purpose was to get parliament to do what parliament should do. For this she received death threats and streams of vitriol. Sadly, it has become the norm for people who disagree with other people's views to receive such threats via "social media". Unbelievable as it might seem, there are nutcases all over the UK and in many other countries who believe that death is appropriate for those who take views opposed to their own. Freedom of speech is under attack even for those who take perfectly reasonable stances.

The "media" which allow these posts should be dealt with by the laws of the land, but neither the police nor any other law enforcement agency seems prepared to deal with them. If these threats were published by newspapers or other mainstream media, editors and publishers would be dealt with severely and, quite likely, heavily fined or imprisoned. The same rules should apply to the heads of the "social media" platforms. They had claimed they were not publishers and therefore not subject to such laws, but that is nonsense – and, to its credit, Facebook finally acknowledged in 2018 that it was indeed a publisher. And early in 2020 the government announced that Ofcom (the oddly named and largely ineffectual Office for Communications) would be given a role in attempting to regulate the social media companies. Good luck with that!

Speaking after the High Court verdict, Ms Miller told the BBC the case was about scrutinising the details of Brexit, such as "how we leave, how they're going to negotiate, the directions of travel the government will take" – all issues which caused Mrs May and her government enormous problems.

She added that the challenge was about more than Brexit. "It is about any government, any prime minister, in the future being able to take away people's rights without consulting parliament," she said. "We cannot have a democracy like that. That isn't a democracy, that is verging on dictatorship." It's what the monarchy used to do and we can't have that again!

The government, somewhat oddly, appealed against the High Court's judgment and the matter went to the Supreme Court which upheld the High Court's decision in December 2016. It was pretty much a foregone conclusion: the government's case was very weak and although it wasn't a unanimous decision by the court, it was a clear one – and so the matter went to parliament, as it should have done without the legal wrangling.

This, however, all worked to Mrs May's advantage. The time taken by the court hearings enabled her to formulate some idea of how to tackle the thorny issues of extricating the UK from the EU. She clearly had little idea how to go about it when she was catapulted into the office of PM after spending six years as a rather mediocre Home Secretary whose talents there were thrown into sharp focus by immigration scandals and other debacles which surfaced under her successor. Mrs May left that office in a state every bit as "unfit for purpose" as when the Labour Home Secretary, John Reid, described it in that way in 2006 (a comment he later attributed to "a senior civil servant").

It was fascinating that after meeting the Queen at Christmas in 2016, the "palace" let it be known that Her Majesty had been disappointed by the lack of information imparted by Mrs May on Brexit issues. This was in sharp contrast to the reaction by the palace after Mr Cameron had announced that the Queen had "purred down the phone" after he rang to let her know the result of the Scottish referendum on independence in November 2014. Apparently it's bad form to say anything about conversations with the UK's Head of State (despite it being a largely ceremonial position) but it doesn't apply the other way round. Mr Cameron apologised both publicly and privately to the monarch. There was no report of a palace apology to Mrs May.

And so the Brexit negotiations got under way. It was all pretty routine stuff which turned strange when the government sought to use a mechanism introduced by Henry VIII to get legislation through by giving ministers extraordinary powers to bypass parliament (again) when transcribing EU edicts into British law. Weird is too weak a word to describe what the government was trying to do.

Incidentally, after the legal wrangling, Mrs May went on to make three major speeches about Brexit – none of them in parliament, thus joining a lengthy list of Prime Ministers who have preferred to ignore parliament (when they can) and talk instead to more sympathetic audiences.

The PM kept repeating the mantra that she was working towards the "smooth and orderly" Brexit that the British people voted for. Did anyone ever meet someone who voted for "smooth and orderly"? Most of those Leave supporters who were quoted in newspapers and in TV and radio interviews claimed they wanted out and didn't care how it happened: it appeared that "rough and disorderly" (although those exact words were not used) would be perfectly acceptable.

After losing a vote on what was known as "her deal" by a huge majority in the House of Commons in January 2019, Mrs May said that "a no-deal exit would betray the referendum result". Quite how she came to that conclusion was not clarified. The referendum campaign didn't go into details of a deal or no deal outcome. Simply "in" or "out".

A further astonishing gaffe was made by Mrs May in a letter sent to the president of the European Commission and others referring to "my parliament". MY parliament. How arrogant could she get? It never was, and never will be, *her* parliament. The Queen refers to "my government" in the drivel the government of the day gives her to read out at each state opening of parliament and there may be some justification for that but for the Prime

Minister to refer to "my parliament" is, if you will pardon the expression, beyond the pale.

Mrs May also never quite got to grips with the question – or the implications – of borders and neither, despite comments to the contrary, had any of the leading outers. The border between the Republic of Ireland and Northern Ireland was always going to be one of the most contentious issues, but the government chose to pretty much ignore it until it became impossible to do so. And the small border between Spain and Gibraltar was also bound to prove a bit of an obstacle. Problems, problems…

Back in November 2016, Boris Johnson had remarked that Britain would make a "titanic success of Brexit". He said: "We are taking the machete of freedom to the brambles of EU regulation. And we are in the process of creating something immensely positive for both sides of the Channel, a new European partnership between a strong UK and a strong EU. Believe me, that's what people of this great continent want to achieve. In the words of our great prime minister, they understand that Brexit means Brexit and we are going to make a titanic success of it." The *Titanic* sank, as we well know, though not without trace. Maybe he meant success of "exceptional strength, size or power" (as the dictionary defines titanic) but who knows? His syntax is often as muddled as his hair.

In July 2018, Mrs May came up with a "policy paper" she believed would form the basis for a solution to all those problems – and proudly declared that her entire cabinet was right behind it. Within a few days it became clear that this was not the case as her lead negotiator (the secretary of state for exiting the EU) and the foreign secretary (aforementioned Boris Johnson) both resigned, as did several junior ministers.

The document was called *The future relationship between the United Kingdom and the European Union.* It proclaimed that: "The United Kingdom will leave the European Union on 29th March 2019 and begin to chart a new course in the world. The government will have delivered on the result of the 2016 referendum – the biggest democratic exercise in this country's history [*an odd claim to make*]. And it will have reached a key milestone in its principal mission – to build a country that works for everyone. A country that is stronger, fairer, more united and more outward-looking." This high-sounding bilge fooled very few, least of all the EU negotiators and the heads of government of member states. So began a frantic round of diplomacy to secure either some sort of deal or no deal at all.

At one point Mrs May was heard demanding respect for her ideas from the EU. Respect can be commanded but never demanded: it has to be earned and earned it was not.

The UK, however, was not alone in its desire to leave the EU. The youthful French President, Emmanuel Macron, told BBC interviewer Andrew Marr in January 2018 that had France held a referendum on membership of the EU after the UK one, the French people would – probably – have voted to leave. So the French people were not going to be given that option.

And the UK had apparently not lost its taste for referenda: in January 2018, an ICM survey, conducted for the *Guardian*, found that 47% (though plus or minus a substantial percentage, remember) of the public backed revisiting the question of EU membership once the terms of Britain's departure were known. The same poll found 34% of voters opposed to it, with roughly a fifth saying they had no opinion on a second referendum.

The pollsters which failed to forecast accurately the result of the referendum – and it's a common failing to be unable to predict the winner of a two-horse race – subsequently told us that it was mainly young people who had voted to stay in and older people who had voted to leave and we were given pretty precise percentages – all of which should be taken not just with a pinch but a whole heap of salt.

It became apparent that many older people liked the free trade arrangements but were less fond of the free movement of people and wider immigration issues, the supremacy of European laws over home-grown ones and the loss of sovereignty of the UK parliament. Younger people cared less about a number of these issues but liked the idea of free movement of people, the opportunities to work in other European countries and the ease of travel throughout the region. They had mixed views on legal matters and sovereignty, possibly because many had been untroubled by such matters.

Mrs May, however, was unable to get anything sorted after months of faffing about and so it became the turn of one Alexander Boris de Pfeffel Johnson to, somehow or other, lead the UK out of the EU, in accordance with what he called the "overwhelming majority" in the referendum. Boris had become well-known for having difficulties in distinguishing fact from fiction and, like the US President, Donald Trump, frequently getting the two mixed up. But the Conservative Party elected him to take on the job and he was able to fulfil a long-held ambition, assisted by one Dominic Cummings, a foul-mouthed "political strategist" who had been campaign director of Vote Leave, and who now hovered Rasputin-like in the background (and sometimes the foreground) of Mr Johnson's team in 10 Downing Street. It's perhaps worth noting that a few weeks after Mr Johnson's victory in the December 2019 general election, Mr Cummings said the civil service needed more weirdos. Maybe he was feeling lonely.

Mr Johnson stated on a number of occasions that the UK would leave the EU on 31st October 2019, no matter what – but that did not happen. He was thwarted at every turn – and deservedly so. Along the way, he had Privy Counsellors mislead the Queen about the reasons for a prorogation of parliament and the prorogation itself was declared illegal by the Supreme Court after Gina Miller (among others) had got involved again. But that just skims the surface of the shenanigans, which could easily be turned into a blockbuster TV series.

The new PM boasted that he had got a new deal from the EU negotiators, even though it was Mrs May's deal with just a few amendments, one being arrangements for Northern Ireland to be treated differently from the rest of the UK, particularly in matters of imports and exports – something that both Mrs May and Mr Johnson had pledged they would never permit. No one seemed to notice that people in the Republic of Ireland, whether there legally or illegally, could, under this deal, move without let or hindrance (the quaint wording in UK passports) into Northern Ireland and on into Britain. Apparently, that was not important.

So, did Mr Johnson resign on 1st November having failed in his attempts to get the UK out of the EU on 31st October? Of course not. Like Mrs May, having taken hold of the reins in No. 10, he was not going to hand them over without a fight.

So, finally, parliament agreed to hold yet another general election – on 12th December 2019.

The rest, as they say, is history ... or almost. The UK did leave the EU on 31st January 2020, though without many meaningful trade deals in place and facing a lengthy period of uncertainty in trying to forge a satisfactory relationship with the EU.

Mr Johnson appeared at that time to be getting on famously with Donald Trump, but the relationship took a knock after the PM announced that he would allow equipment made by a Chinese telecommunications company, Huawei, to be used in the UK's 5G networks. This, according to reports, elicited an apoplectic reaction from said President, who might just have recalled what had been said about him by Boris while he was Mayor of London. Calling Donald Trump a person of "quite stupefying ignorance that makes him, frankly, unfit to hold the office" was hardly calculated to encourage a long-term and friendly relationship leading to the wonderful trade deal that both leaders said they wanted post-Brexit.

In July 2018, the perceptive former US President Barack Obama referred to Boris Johnson as the British version of Donald Trump. Perhaps that was unfair. Mr Johnson could not be described as stupefyingly ignorant although as a porky-teller and a womaniser he does appear to be from the same mould. There are other similarities: both were born in New York, both have short attention spans and pay little attention to detail, both speak ill-advisedly, and both have more money than they know what to do with. That might or might not bode well for what is known as the "special relationship" between the US and UK upon which a successful outcome of Brexit is said to be so dependent.

And then came coronavirus…

Great days for fearless newspapers

It became clear within a few months of the referendum that the fearless newspapers of this fair land would seek to outdo each other with the ridiculous or absurd wording of their front-page headlines.

For instance, after the Supreme Court ruling in November 2016, the *Daily Mail* put "Enemies Of The People" in huge type alongside photos of some of the judges. This was certainly the most moronic headline to have appeared, at least until the last day of July 2018 when the *Daily Express* gave it some competition with "How Dare He Insult 17M Brexit Voters". This referred to some comments by Lord Mandelson, a former Labour cabinet minister and European Commissioner, who twice resigned from said cabinet over some dodgy dealings (although the first time in particular he claimed to have done nothing wrong) and could hardly be considered worthy of such a headline.

Onlookers (me mostly) did, however, judge that very highly in terms of moronicity (it's necessary, unfortunately, to make up a word or two in speaking about the extraordinary stupidity of some of the tabloids). However, as it was really a rant rather than a headline (though the same could perhaps be said of the *Daily Mail*'s outburst) it scored slightly lower on the moronicity scale.

So, to the *Daily Mail* goes the honour – just – of publishing the stupidest, most moronic post-referendum headline. In terms of stupidity it was right up there with the *Sunday Sport*'s ludicrous "World War 2 Bomber Found on Moon" headline in 1988 – but at least the *Sunday Sport* had never pretended to be a serious newspaper.

Meanwhile, to those Leave-supporting newspapers and others who claimed the Supreme Court judges had declared war on democracy, you were clearly right up there on the moronic scale; this award, however, was restricted to headlines.

It all brings to mind that brilliant poem by Humbert Wolfe (1885-1940), the Italian-born English civil servant and literary critic:

You cannot hope to bribe or twist,
thank God! the British journalist.
But, seeing what the man will do
unbribed, there's no occasion to.

"Fake news" is certainly nothing new and "social media" shouldn't take all the credit for it.

The 1975 referendum: a look back...

On 5th June 1975, voters in the UK took part in "The United Kingdom European Communities (EC) Membership Referendum", often referred to as the Common Market referendum or EEC membership referendum. This was the first nationwide referendum ever held and was intended to gauge support for the country's continued membership of the European Communities which it had entered on 1st January 1973 under the Conservative government of Edward Heath.

Just over 67% of the voters – a respectable margin – opted to stay in the Common Market, despite several cabinet ministers having come out in favour of British withdrawal.

The result, which followed Labour's commitment to hold such a vote in its general election manifesto the previous October, was hailed by the Prime Minister, Harold Wilson, as an "historic decision".

The question asked was: "Do you think the UK should stay in the European Community (Common Market)?" Most of the 68 administrative counties and regions in Great Britain and Northern Ireland voted in favour with only Shetland and the Western Isles voting against.

The Home Secretary, Roy Jenkins, commented: "It puts the uncertainty behind us. It commits Britain to Europe; it commits us to playing an active, constructive and enthusiastic role in it." The Conservatives, led by Margaret Thatcher, had also campaigned to stay in the Common Market and the former leader, Edward Heath, said he was delighted with the result.

Members of the "No" campaign promised to work constructively within the EEC. The Industry Secretary, Tony Benn, who had been opposed to the Common Market, said: "When the British people speak, everyone, including Members of Parliament, should tremble before their decision and that's certainly the spirit with which I accept the result of the referendum."

Things were a little different 41 years later.

A club to keep clear of ... perhaps

While it is clear that, whatever one's political opinions, there is much to regret about the referendum, its conduct and aftermath, there are numerous valid reasons to be sceptical of the EU.

• The extent of corruption in Europe costs the EU economy about £100 billion a year, said a statement from the European Commission in February 2014. A survey conducted for the commission discovered that nearly half the companies doing business in Europe had experienced problems. Nearly all companies in Greece, Spain and Italy believed corruption was widespread while it was considered rare in Finland and Sweden. The European home affairs commissioner at the time said corruption was "eroding trust in democracy", adding that there was no "corruption-free zone" in Europe. The UK was criticised in the commission's report for failing to clean up and regulate the financing of political parties – a major factor in corruption, according to the commission. One section of the report which dealt with corruption in EU institutions and funds, following the annual refusal of the European Court of Auditors to sign off the accounts, was dropped from the published statement.

• In a substantial report (running to 496 pages) published by the EU's commissioner for social affairs in January 2014 – entitled "Employment and social developments in Europe 2013" – a warning was given that the euro was fuelling inequality and the loss of sovereignty entailed in eurozone membership had led to increased unemployment and social hardship in many countries. It said that deepening economic divisions between north and south, and rich and poor eurozone countries threatened to undermine the European Union.

• Being a Member of the European Parliament (MEP) has been a nice little earner for a good many people across the EU – though MEPs from the UK have, by government decree, been treated less well. Some from other nations have reported that they can clear a million euros tax free during a five-year term without breaking any rules. MEPs are paid (in 2018) €102,000 a year (taxed at the "community" rate of 22% which applies to all EU officials) but also get staff allowances and other entitlements of more than €400,000, which includes €100,000 in "general expenditure" and "daily subsistence" that is paid tax-free and without the need to produce any receipts or give any details of how the money is used. The European Court of Justice has ruled that it would be a breach of the privacy of individual MEPs if details of their expenses were made public.

• It is hard to deny that a common currency across EU countries is basically a good idea. The name "euro" was formally adopted in 1995 and launched in 1999 as an invisible currency, used only for accounting purposes; the actual currency, i.e. banknotes and coins, was not introduced until 1st January 2002. The EU Commission had – rather unusually for this august body – laid down a number of sensible criteria, "euro convergence criteria", which countries had to comply with before they could be considered suitable to adopt the currency. Unfortunately, as the launch drew nearer, it looked as if barely a handful of countries would meet the criteria, so some creative accounting was encouraged to ensure a "successful" start. This was fine while economies were growing but when a downturn came, that creativity proved to be disastrous and a number of countries had to be bailed out, Greece being the most notable. Part of the disaster was caused by the EU's insistence on a common interest rate, set by the European Central Bank, being applied across the "eurozone". This was, not unusually for the European bigwigs, a stupid and economically illiterate decision which was bound to cause serious problems, particularly with the less developed economies. For the record, the first adopters of the euro were Austria, Belgium, France, Germany, Ireland, Italy, Luxembourg, Portugal, Spain and The Netherlands. Greece was accepted in 2001, just in time for the launch of the actual currency. The UK and Denmark negotiated opt-outs, but since the launch other countries have joined and by 2019 there were 19 EU member countries, plus a half-dozen or so non-member countries, using the euro.

Regulation
The regulators

What do they do? Are they necessary?

One of the UK's growth sectors in recent years has been in "regulation". Regulatory bodies have existed in various forms for many years but a golden era for them was ushered in during Margaret Thatcher's privatisation binge in the 1980s and 90s.

It was her intention that the new regulators would exist for only as long as necessary to ensure a smooth transition of the industries from the public to the private sector and for competition to replace the state monopolies. More than 30 years later many of these regulators have become bloated bureaucracies doing all they can to ensure their survival, spending more and more money and employing ever greater numbers of people.

One word that keeps cropping up when you look for information about the various regulators is "independent". This word appears to be used in much the same way that dictatorships insert the word "democratic" into the names of their countries. And it is rare for any of the bodies to explain who they are independent from.

In a shortish book such as this it would be practically impossible to give details of all of the regulatory bodies in existence but it is worth looking at some of them to examine how they function and what they achieve – which in many cases is not very much. To be fair, some probably are essential and some do perform worthwhile tasks; but all of them are full of praise for their own activities and "achievements", as can be seen from their beautifully presented annual reports – which to a cynical observer might seem to be the high points of their years.

While many people believe that a large proportion of the country's regulations are the "fault" of the EU, that is simply not the case. The majority are home-grown, although it is true that many have been amended to fit in with European requirements.

What follows includes details of some of the considerable number of regulators that can affect various aspects of our lives – and others that have little or no effect but exist at the whim of officialdom.

This list does not include the regulators of professional bodies – such as the General Medical Council, the General Dental Council, the Royal College of Veterinary Surgeons, Nursing & Midwifery Council, Health & Care Professions Council, Royal Pharmaceutical Society of Great Britain, and those in many other fields such as engineering – which maintain registers of the people allowed to practise in particular fields and generally have disciplinary powers designed to deal with cases of malpractice or professional misconduct.

Reports on some regulators appear in later chapters, such as media and money; but let us start with the utility regulators – water, gas and electricity, telephones and other forms of communication – and follow on with railways and the roads, health and safety (everyone's favourite), the environment, data protection, gambling, competition, trading standards, charities, elections, aspects of healthcare, and numerous others, some of them more niche and quirky than others, before concluding with a report on a link-up by various regulators and a code which is meant to regulate how the regulators operate.

No competition – but a regulator imposed anyway

OfWat (Office of Water Service originally but now Water Services Regulation Authority) describes itself as "The economic regulator of the water sector in England and Wales". It aims, says its website, to "work with others for the benefit of customers of water and wastewater services and wider society in England and Wales both now and in the future".

It is a non-ministerial government department (these are headed by senior civil servants and not ministers and usually have a regulatory or inspection function) established in 1989 when the water and sewerage industry in England and Wales was privatised.

It is led by a chairman plus a chief executive, along with six non-executive directors, a senior director of finance and governance, a senior director of "water 2020" (whatever that might mean) and a senior director of strategy and planning.

Then there is its "executive", comprising the chief executive, the senior director of finance and governance and the senior director of "water 2020", plus a senior director of business improvement, a senior director of corporate communications, a senior director of customers and casework, a chief economist, a senior director of Thames Tideway and a senior director of strategy and planning – all fine-sounding and no doubt highly-paid jobs for a fairly small task that is funded by licence fees which are "recovered" from the water companies.

Its "vision", as stated on the website, "is to be working at the leading edge, trusted and respected, challenging ourselves and others to build trust and confidence in water". On the front cover of its 2018-19 annual report are the words "Trust in water", whatever that might mean.

In the financial year which ended on 31st March 2017, OfWat had 190 staff, up from 171 the previous year, plus 13 agency staff and consultants, down from 34. Income exceeded £22 million with nearly £14 million of that allocated to "staff" costs and fees. In 2018-19 staff costs rose to £18.68 million. A splendid rate of expansion.

An article in the *Independent* in April 2018 stated: "OfWat, which had given every impression of being the Office for Doing Not Very Much, has outlined a package of measures it wants to take to bring the embattled sector 'back in balance'."

Some of the measures, the article continued, amounted to wagging its finger at the industry and telling it to do what it should have been doing for years.

It may be hard for some of us to understand why it is deemed necessary for OfWat to exist at all. Most of the "watchdogs" established during the Thatcher era of privatisation were intended to smooth the transition from public to private ownership and to ensure free and fair competition. As there is no competition whatsoever in the water industry, the only job for OfWat was to ensure the former – a simple and hardly time-consuming job. But, like many bodies set up with a simple remit, it gradually expanded its activities to give the impression of being indispensable. It isn't!

OfWat is just for England and Wales. The Water Commissioner for Scotland regulates Scottish water supplies; The Utility Regulator is responsible for regulating the electricity, gas, water and sewerage industries in Northern Ireland where it claims "to promote the short- and long-term interests of consumers".

The Consumer Council for Water (CCWater) represents domestic and business customers in England and Wales, with regard to costs, value for money and quality of service. It is "independent" of both the water industry and the regulator and investigates customer complaints which have not been resolved by the water company concerned.

Three separate authorities – the Environment Agency in England and Wales, Scottish Environment Protection Agency in Scotland and the Environment and Heritage Service in Northern Ireland – have responsibility for monitoring environmental effects, conserving water resources and controlling and preventing pollution. Quite a remit.

Then there is the Drinking Water Inspectorate, another so-called "independent" government regulator for England and Wales; in Scotland it is the responsibility of the Scottish Executive to regulate drinking water and in Northern Ireland the Northern Ireland Water Service looks after it.

That, overall, is a mighty lot of regulation completely separate from OfWat. Would anyone notice, apart from its staff, if it was washed away? And surely some of the other bodies could be combined to reduce the bureaucracy, save money and be rather more effective.

Intriguingly, in March 2019 Ofwat produced a document on "reducing regulatory burdens" – but entirely failed to mention the most obvious one: its own closure.

Some 'protection' for gas and electricity consumers

Ofgem is the Office of Gas and Electricity Markets, another non-ministerial government department and an "independent" national regulatory authority. Its principal stated objective is "to protect the interests of existing and future electricity and gas consumers" and its logo includes the words, "Making a positive difference for energy consumers". It was formed by the merger of the Office of Electricity Regulation (OFFER – a non-ministerial government department established in 1989) and the Office of Gas Supply (Ofgas – set up in 1996).

It is governed by the Gas and Electricity Markets Authority (GEMA) which consists of non-executive and executive members and a non-executive chairperson and whose members are appointed by the Secretary of State at the Department for Business, Energy and Industrial Strategy.

Funding for Ofgem comes from the companies that it regulates, which are required to pay an annual licence fee, and it claims to be wholly independent of those companies.

Its budget for 2016-17 was just under £91 million but it requested additional capital funding from the government to enable a move to plush new offices in Canary Wharf. Two years later income had risen to £96.73 million and spending to £97.16 million.

The regulator had 971 staff in 2016-17, up from 907 the year before, with staff costs accounting for more than £59 million of its income in that financial year. In 2018-19, staff costs were £61.31 million.

The original privatisation of the "electricity supply" was a long-drawn-out and pretty muddled affair. It was the Electricity Act 1989 which provided for the privatisation of the electricity industry in Great Britain and a year later the Central Electricity Generating Board began to be privatised with its assets divided among three new companies: Powergen, National Power and National Grid Company. Later, the nuclear component within National Power was removed and vested in another state-owned company, Nuclear Electric.

The Scottish industry was privatised in 1991 and the Northern Ireland one in 1992, followed a year later by the supply industry there.

In 1995 the major assets of Nuclear Electric and Scottish Nuclear were merged with the UK's eight most advanced nuclear plants, forming a new private company, British Energy.

Finally, in 2001, the Central Electricity Generating Board was formally wound up.

In 2007, Northern Ireland generators were told to sell their electricity into the Single Electricity Market, an all-island market with the Republic of Ireland from which suppliers purchase electricity at a single market rate. As we've already seen with respect to the water industry, Northern Ireland also has The Utility Regulator, which is responsible for regulating the electricity, gas, water and sewerage industries there.

And after becoming the UK's largest electricity generation company, British Energy was bought, in 2009, by Électricité de France (EDF), a state-owned company.

When Mrs Thatcher's government decided to privatise the gas industry, she was informed, by the banks and other advisers who would be making huge sums out of helping the government achieve its aims, that gas was being sold to consumers at too low a price to make the initial share offering attractive to investors. So the PM decreed that, for the three years prior to privatisation, gas prices would rise annually by 10% above the rate of inflation. After those three years the price to consumers had risen by well over 40% and the advisers considered that would be sufficient for them to make another killing. And so it was.

There were many who wondered how long it would be before the directors of the new companies trumpeted the success of privatisation by crowing that they had been able to hold prices at the privatisation level – or even reduce them. It took less than three years and was hardly a great achievement as most six-year-olds could have done it. And, fortunately, there was still plenty in the kitty to allow the companies' top executives to offer lucrative directorships (often non-executive) to former ministers and senior civil servants who had overseen the privatisation, thus enabling them to enrich themselves, often substantially. This happened following other privatisations as well but was not considered by officialdom to be corrupt, even though it gave every impression of being so.

So, the gas industry was now in private hands, British Gas Plc was formed out of the dreadful state-owned British Gas and Ofgas was set up to "regulate" the industry.

In 1990, the National Grid was formed and, in 1994, British Gas was restructured and Transco created to transport and store gas. Three years later British Gas was split into separate companies, Centrica Plc and BG Plc. A further three years on, Lattice Group (the parent of Transco) split from BG Plc and then in 2002 Lattice Group merged with the National Grid to form National Grid Transco plc. Hope that's all clear. Whatever British Gas now is celebrated its 200th anniversary in 2012.

Then, in 2009, "smart meters" were introduced. Ofgem claims these will transform the competitive energy markets and help create a smarter energy system fit for the future, with gas and electricity suppliers required to take all reasonable steps to install them in all domestic and small business premises by the end of 2020.

It's one of the finest examples one can imagine of appearing to do something useful without achieving very much at all. Accompanied by an advertising campaign urging us all "to get Gaz and Leccy under control" – which should at least get an award for banality – these meters indicate how much gas and electricity is being used at any one time.

According to Ofgem (which is backed up in its claims by the Department of Energy & Climate Change, which became part of the Department for Business, Energy & Industrial Strategy in July 2016) they should help reduce the demand for energy. There is, however, little to indicate that this might happen. What they actually do is feed meter readings back to the supply companies so that they will be able to reduce, substantially, their need for people to go door-to-door reading meters. So, what is promoted as being of benefit to consumers is actually of greatest benefit to the companies which supply them. A neat twist.

The Department of Energy & Climate Change (DECC) claims that it is working to make sure the UK has secure, clean, affordable energy supplies. So what need is there for Ofgem as well? Who knows? Ofgem does have some teeth and since 2010 has imposed more than £100 million in fines and redress levies against energy suppliers, including, in 2014, a £12 million redress levy on E.ON in May as well as a somewhat pathetic £1 million redress levy on British Gas in July. Nevertheless, the gas and electricity companies can do pretty much as they wish and, despite objections from politicians, consumers and Ofgem, they keep putting up prices and giving some pretty rotten deals to customers.

Getting the 'best' from 'communications'

"Making communications work for everyone" is the fine-sounding but nonsensical strapline of Ofcom, which describes itself as "the communications regulator in the UK". Its stated task is "to regulate the TV, radio and video-on-demand sectors, fixed-line telecoms (phones), mobiles and postal services, plus the airwaves over which wireless devices operate".

A statement on its website reads: "We make sure that people in the UK get the best from their communications services and are protected from scams and sharp practices, while ensuring that competition can thrive." And in its annual reports, it says its values are: "Excellence, Collaboration, Agility, Empowerment" – whatever that might mean.

Ofcom was established as a body corporate by the Office of Communications Act 2002; and The Communications Act 2003 says that Ofcom's principal duty is to further the interests of citizens and of consumers, where appropriate by promoting competition.

It is funded by fees from the industry for regulating broadcasting and communications networks, along with grant-in-aid from the government, and in the year ended 31st March 2017 its total income was in excess of £140 million. Spending was close to £139 million, including £68.5 million on staff. The average number of employees (described as full-time equivalents) in that year was given as 828, up from 795 the previous year. Two years later it had income closer to £200 million and had an operating deficit of more than £230 million, having spent £232 million on legal costs; staff costs had risen to more than £76 million. Quite an enterprise – and one with an expanding remit (*see further on about its "regulatory role" with the "independent" BBC and a government proposal early in 2020 that it should have some power over social media companies*).

Ofcom's main decision-making body is its board, which is said to provide strategic direction for the organisation. This has a non-executive chairman and deputy chairman, various executive directors (including the chief executive), and several non-executive directors. There is also a policy and management board (nine members), a content board (a committee of the main board which "sets and enforces quality and standards for television and radio") and various committees and advisory bodies.

The actual work is led by senior directors in Glasgow, Cardiff, Belfast and London (the head office). An England Regions team is based in London and an Advisory Committee for England "advises Ofcom about the interests and opinions, in relation to communications and postal matters, of persons living in England".

In Cardiff, the Ofcom Wales team "represents Ofcom in Wales and Wales within Ofcom" (to use Ofcom's quaint expression) – managing relationships and communications with the general public and a wide range of industry stakeholders, including politicians, industry and the media.

In the same vein, the Ofcom team in Belfast "represents Ofcom in Northern Ireland and Northern Ireland in Ofcom" – and also has responsibility for the Isle of Man; while the Ofcom Scotland Team "represents Ofcom in Scotland and Scotland in Ofcom".

So that, in brief, is how the whole thing is structured.

In April 2017, Ofcom's remit was increased to "regulate" or act as watchdog of the BBC (under the terms of the new Royal Charter for the BBC which came into effect at the beginning of 2017) – the latter role having previously been handled by the now defunct BBC Trust. It's hard to deny that the BBC Trust, which replaced the BBC's board of governors in 2007, was pretty useless at holding the BBC to account for anything it broadcast or for how the corporation was run, but it was quite a radical decision for the government to remove one of the main foundations of the BBC's long-cherished (by itself, at least) independence.

Part of Ofcom's new remit was to look at the BBC's impact on competition, something the BBC had studiously ignored while regularly engaging in anti-competitive activities. *But that, along with the BBC's other activities, deserves a separate chapter.*

It was a fresh challenge for Ofcom's content board which, as stated earlier, "sets and enforces quality and standards for television and radio". How, for instance, does that board reconcile that task with the pornographic content on satellite systems? Content which would likely – and rightly – be considered illegal if disseminated in any other way is apparently deemed acceptable when distributed via satellite. The worst of it has to be paid for on top of normal subscription fees but there are 10-minute sessions freely available to anyone who looks in. If the content board considers the "quality and standard" of such material to be OK, what hope is there for the "regulation" of anything else? Maybe Ofcom is powerless to interfere in this – but what is the purpose of "regulation" if that is the case?

And just how effective is Ofcom at regulating the activities of the telecoms companies? The greatest problem this writer encountered in moving house and business in 2016 was with three telecoms companies: TalkTalk, Unicom and British Telecom. All were required to carry out relatively straightforward tasks in closing down services at one house in Surrey and, apart from TalkTalk, getting them going again at another residence. If they were given marks out of 10 for what they did, all would be way down on the negative scale: *minus* 100 at least for TalkTalk which wanted to keep charging for lines it had agreed to disconnect and had the temerity to instruct a debt collection agency to pursue payment of a non-existent charge (before finally giving up); *minus* 150 for Unicom which got almost everything wrong and, despite assurances of reduced costs, sent in the biggest bill we'd ever received, including charging for the installation of four lines when only two were required and installed; and *minus* 150 for BT whose only task was to transfer its broadband service but which took four months to complete the task, after sending engineers to the house we'd moved from on three separate occasions. Appalling service all round in an industry that we are told is well-regulated. And, from regular columns in weekend newspapers and elsewhere, it's clear that many others suffer similarly bad treatment from these supposedly well-regulated suppliers.

Ofcom, of course, has a nifty disclaimer: "Parliament has not given us powers to resolve individual people's complaints about their broadband, home phone or mobile phone. Instead, these can be considered by alternative 'dispute resolution' services." Oddly, however, it does deal with individual complaints about TV and radio.

The bloated and expensive bureaucracy that is Ofcom needs to pull its socks up if it is to get anywhere near "making communications work for everyone".

For instance, have you tried buying a telephone from an O2 shop? We went into one in Surrey to get a phone with a larger keypad than normal. We found an ideal one which had a price tag of about £43. But when we tried to buy it, the young smart alec behind the counter said we had to pay another £10 for a sim card – something we neither wanted nor needed. He insisted we couldn't buy the phone unless we paid the additional £10 "as it is company policy".

Eventually, after a lengthy conversation over O2's website, we got the phone for the £43 and transferred the sim card from the phone we were replacing. The question arises as to whether this is a matter for Ofcom or Trading Standards? Shops have the power to refuse custom but are required to sell goods at the price shown (unless there has been an obvious mistake) – and there was no notice visible that a £10 surcharge would be applied. It's a straightforward breach of consumer law but O2 has continued to get away with it. All that regulation but no one actually doing very much to help consumers!

And as a reward for being pretty hopeless, the government of Boris Johnson announced in February 2020 that it was "minded" (great word!) to appoint Ofcom to oversee social media companies – although not with any great powers to actually do anything other than impose some derisory fines or "name and shame" some executives of the companies concerned. Those companies had already raised objections to a proposal that they should be charged a levy to fund Ofcom's work.

As Nat King Cole crooned in the early 1960s, "There may be trouble ahead."

Keeping us all on the right lines…

The Office of Rail and Road describes itself as an independent regulator and an independent statutory body. Under the strapline "Protecting the interests of rail and road users", it has a board, whose members are appointed by the Secretary of State for Transport for a fixed term of up to five years, which is responsible for setting strategy and overseeing its delivery, and "a team of executive directors" responsible for delivering the board's objectives and business plan, in line with the office's legal duties. It has six offices: in London, Birmingham, Bristol, Glasgow, Manchester and York – with no office space apparently required in Wales or Northern Ireland.

The board is led by a "chair" and includes the chief executive, six non-executive directors, along with the director of railway markets and economics, the chief inspector of railways, the director of railway planning and performance, plus a member of the audit committee.

The staff is divided into directorates led by the executive directors, with the titles of: chief executive; director of strategy and policy (to develop and implement ORR's policy and strategy for regulation of the rail sector); director of communications (responsible for ORR's relations with staff, stakeholders and the media and for explaining the value ORR brings to transport and the economy in the UK – which must be a near impossible remit); director of corporate operations and organisational development; director of railway markets and economics (monitoring Network Rail); director of legal services; director of railway safety (the chief inspector of railways and responsible for the work of the Railway Safety Directorate); and director of planning and performance (with the emphasis on *railway* planning and performance).

A quick glance at that list of board members and directorates indicates how heavily weighted it is towards looking after the railways, with scarcely a mention of roads. And, if all that effort is going into the railways, one might question why rail services are so often poor, or atrocious, and why there is such a muddle – and a serious lack of competition. Most of the competition is about seeing which companies can outbid others for the franchises that can be handed out to them by the Department for Transport, or taken back by the department if they get their figures wrong! Maybe it's because the department is so heavily involved ... but that's a tale for separate discussion.

There is, however, a highways committee among the four committees which report to the board, the others being the audit and risk committee, the remuneration and nominations committee and the health and safety regulation committee. The highways committee is said to advise the ORR board "in developing an appropriate and effective monitoring framework and internal decision-making framework for roads; and acts as a forum for policy development with senior staff".

Pretty vague stuff, as so often in matters of regulation.

So what does ORR do? In its own words, "We regulate the rail industry's health and safety performance, we hold Network Rail and High Speed 1 (HS1) to account and we make sure that the rail industry is competitive and fair. We are also the monitor of Highways England and we have economic regulatory functions in relation to railways in Northern Ireland and for the northern half of the Channel Tunnel, situated in the UK."

On strategy, it says: "Our long-term vision for the mainline railway industry is a partnership of Network Rail, operators, suppliers and funders working together to deliver a safe, high performing, efficient and developing railway."

It is funded by the rail industry through licence fees and safety levies. Its economic regulation activities are funded almost entirely through Network Rail's licence fee and it also recovers costs for its work relating to other networks not owned by Network Rail. Health and safety activities are funded through a safety levy, which is based on the turnover of each railway service provider.

No regulation of HS2

While ORR is responsible for oversight of HS1 – the Channel Tunnel Rail Link (a 108-kilometre high-speed railway between London and the UK end of the Channel Tunnel), which would appear to require an absolute minimum of regulation – it has nothing to do with HS2, the scheme for linking London by high-speed rail to various parts of the north of England, starting with Birmingham and then moving on to Manchester, Sheffield and elsewhere. The budget for this began, at 2015 prices, at £55.7 billion – and in the grand tradition of infrastructure and other major government projects within the UK, is likely to end up being a great deal more. *More on this later.*

The responsibility for "developing and promoting" this network has been given to High Speed Two (HS2) Ltd, an executive non-departmental public body, sponsored by the Department for Transport and funded by grant-in-aid from the government. In the year ended 31st March 2017, £537 million was spent on "preparatory work", which was actually 30% less than had been allocated. So far, so good.

The stated objectives of HS2 Ltd are (or were): first, to design, build and operate to the highest safety standards; second, to build and operate sustainably, responsibly and respectfully of the communities, wildlife and places it affects; and third, to build a reliable, seamless and easy-to-use system for all passengers and well-integrated with existing transport systems. It may well have done OK on the first, but has been hopeless on the second and has no hope of getting anywhere near achieving the third.

There was inadequate scrutiny of proposals right from the start; grossly inadequate supervision of HS2's work; inadequate consultation on every aspect of the second objective; a refusal to listen to any alternatives; a flat refusal to make any effort to link with Heathrow airport (even though it heads out from London in that direction) – which would have been useful "integration"; and so on. As a result, the UK will eventually have a high-speed rail network of sorts, at vast cost: but it could all have been done so much better with proper attention to detail and genuine efforts to achieve the objectives listed above.

Might it have been better if ORR had been given oversight? Despite the shortcomings of this regulator, it might well have been. This is one area where effective regulation and oversight could have been beneficial.

There have been some remarkable incidents along the way. One of the more memorable came in July 2017, when the Minister for Transport, Chris Grayling, announced £6.6 billion worth of contracts for building Phase 1 of

HS2. Among the companies awarded contracts was Carillion, which at the time was well-known to be in deep financial doo-dah. Its troubles had been fully documented in newspapers and elsewhere (no Minister or senior civil servant could have missed it, not even in a department so detached from reality as this one) and its share price had plummeted. So what better company to get involved in this enormous project!

A short time later (January 2018), it went into liquidation. This led to questions in parliament – during Prime Minister's Questions, Theresa May defended the government's decision to award the contracts by saying: "We were a customer of Carillion, not the manager of Carillion."

This may well go down, despite stiff competition, as one of the stupidest responses ever given to a question in the House of Commons by a Prime Minister.

Note, too, a statement by Chris Grayling at the time of the announcement of these first contracts: "It is inconceivable that the cost of HS2 will spiral out of control." It might as well have been a line from a pantomime, as it is easy to imagine the audience responding, "Oh no it isn't."

Soon after construction work got under way, it was announced that trains wouldn't be running as fast as promised and that there wouldn't be as many of them as first stated. Not a good start for this ill-thought-out and ludicrously expensive project. By the time Boris Johnson's new administration announced a review of the entire project in August 2019, the hapless Mr Grayling had, by this time, been removed from the department.

Then, in September 2019, the government announced that "the first phase of HS2 between London Euston and Birmingham could be delayed by five years until 2031 with the costs rising to between £81 billion and £88 billion". Who could have guessed it? A few months later, the figure had passed the £100 billion mark – just about double the price announced five years earlier. Quite an achievement. The line will extend to some 330 miles (or more eventually) so that's well over £300 million per mile of track.

Despite any nagging doubts, however, the whole scheme was given the go-ahead by Boris Johnson in February 2020, though completion could be well over 20 years away. And by then the price may well have doubled again.

A regulated monopoly

The railways, as users well know, provide very mixed levels of service. The Department of Transport has made a pig's ear of the franchising system and Network Rail which tells us that it owns and operates the railway infrastructure in England, Wales and Scotland *on behalf of the nation* – all 20,000 miles of track, 30,000 bridges and viaducts and thousands of tunnels, signals, level crossings and points – but it does what might be termed a pretty mediocre job even though it describes itself as "a passenger and customer focused business".

Network Rail is a public company, limited by guarantee, officially a state-controlled not-for-profit (or not-for-dividend, as it says in its annual report) operation which was classified in 2014 as a "public sector company that operates as a regulated monopoly". Public sector bodies are subject to direct parliamentary scrutiny and accountability and Network Rail is answerable to the Department for Transport and Transport Scotland. The majority of its funding comes from the government.

The ORR says it "makes sure we meet the needs of our customers, passengers and freight users, as well as being a good neighbour to the 22 million people living or working within 500 metres of the railway". Furthermore, it says, the ORR "determines that we spend efficiently the income we receive from the government and the outputs we must deliver during each five-year control period". The chief executive "is personally accountable to parliament for Network Rail's stewardship of the public funds it receives". Network Rail is also subject to the ORR's regulation for its health and safety performance and for management of the network consistent with its network licence.

Network Rail was set up following the fiasco of Railtrack, which had been set up in 1994 after the privatisation of British Rail. Railtrack was actually a group of companies that owned pretty much what Network Rail does now. It was a massive operation and was in the FTSE 100 Index. But it experienced major financial problems and in 2002 most of it was transferred to Network Rail – effectively a renationalisation – leaving shareholders with worthless stock, though part of Railtrack was transferred to a new business, RT Group plc, which limped along until 2010.

One of Network Rail's first big projects was, naturally, to build itself swish new headquarters in Milton Keynes which it moved into in 2012. Subsequently, the company gained well-deserved notoriety for paying substantial bonuses to already well-paid executives for achieving not very much.

In June 2015 the government announced significant changes at Network Rail "because in some areas performance had fallen below the standards expected" (a pretty radical if understated comment from the government of the day) and to reflect the amended accountability arrangements following its reclassification as a public sector company.

In the 2016-17 financial year Network Rail had revenues of £6.76 billion and recorded a pre-tax surplus of £483 million, but had debts of £46.5 billion, up nearly £5 billion on the previous year. In the five years to March 2019, the company received some £19.6 billion from the government. It employs more than 35,000 people, about three-quarters of whom work on operating and maintaining the railways.

At the very least it provides a considerable challenge for the ORR. There's a delightful and revealing paragraph in the company's annual report for 2016-17, headed "Cost of service". This reads: "The ORR considers what costs an efficiently run business would incur to operate and maintain our network for each year of each control period. They vary and can include, for example, costs relating to employees, office rental, information technology systems and taxes. The regulator determines what it considers to be an efficient cost and this may be different to the actual costs we incur." Brilliant.

Monitoring the performance of roads

From 1st April 2015, ORR was given new responsibilities for monitoring the efficiency and performance of England's strategic road network, this work to be funded by the Department for Transport. In both 2016-17 and 2017-18, the Global Competitiveness Index published by the World Economic Forum ranked the UK's roads at 27th in the world for their quality, behind most Western European and Scandinavian countries and many in the Middle East. The UK was ranked behind countries such as Croatia, Malaysia and Chile – this despite the fact that motorists in the UK pay some of the highest tax rates in the world to run their vehicles – so there should be plenty of scope for ORR to bring about improvements.

For the record, in the 2018-19 financial year, the ORR had income of £31.391 million and spent £31.394 million (remarkably close: as in other cases, it's almost as though the organisation felt obliged to spend all its income in order to justify it). Staff costs amounted to £22.435 million: the organisation employs about 300 people.

Overseeing health and safety in the workplace

The Health and Safety Executive (HSE), an executive non-departmental public body sponsored by the Department for Work and Pensions, is the national independent regulator for health and safety in the workplace. This includes private or publicly-owned health and social care settings in Great Britain.

It works in partnership with co-regulators in local authorities to inspect, investigate and where necessary take enforcement action.

The government says it acts in the public interest to reduce work-related death and serious injury across Great Britain's workplaces. It is also the "competent authority" for biocides, pesticides, detergents and industrial chemicals.

It states that: "We ensure our regulation stays proportionate, consistent, modern and effective. We seek to make legislation easier to understand without reducing standards, and aim to improve dutyholder performance and compliance."

The HSE is led by a non-executive board which sets the organisation's long-term direction, strategy and objectives. The delivery of these, along with day-to-day management, is the responsibility of the chief executive and a management board.

It is responsible for enforcing health and safety at workplaces including: factories; farms; building sites; mines; schools and colleges; fairgrounds; gas, electricity and water systems; hospitals and nursing homes; central and local government premises; and offshore installations. However, local authority environmental health departments are responsible for premises such as offices (except government offices), shops, hotels, restaurants, leisure premises, nurseries and playgroups, pubs and clubs, privately-owned museums, places of worship, sheltered accommodation and care homes.

In its annual report for 2016-17, the HSE said that it "is founded upon fair, proportionate, consistent and well-targeted regulatory practice. Failure to deliver an effective regulatory function would have a significant impact and we must not be complacent in continuing to regulate to the highest of standards."

In the same year, HSE employed roughly 2,500 people, costing close to £140.7 million out of total operating expenditure of £224.1 million. Income from fees and charges during the year totalled £61.06 million with taxpayer-funded income of £140 million. Unusually for a regulator of this size, staff costs were similar two years later.

Intriguingly, there were 28 accidents involving HSE staff in 2016-17, with a further 171 "incidents" and 65 cases of ill health. It would seem the regulator is not very good at regulating itself.

Perhaps surprisingly, HSE states that it does not answer general health and safety questions and suggests people engage the services of a health and safety consultant via the Occupational Safety and Health Consultants Register (OSHCR), a register of consultants who can offer general advice to UK businesses to help them manage health and safety risks.

However, it also advises that: "If you have a specific question on how the health and safety law applies to a particular issue at your workplace, for which HSE is the enforcing authority and you cannot find the answer on our website, then you can ask us by completing the online advice form. We aim to respond within 30 working days." Who would dare to suggest that a month seems a long time to answer a specific question!

The HSE, as we have seen, covers Great Britain. Northern Ireland has its own arrangements: The Health and Safety Executive for Northern Ireland (HSENI) is an executive non-departmental public body sponsored by the Department for the Economy (DfE). It is the lead body responsible for the promotion and enforcement of health and safety at work standards in Northern Ireland and has both a "vision" and a "mission", the former being, "To achieve world-class performance in workplace health and safety and therefore improve the overall economic and social well being of our community"; and the latter, "To ensure that risks to people's health and safety arising from work activities are effectively controlled."

Taking action, or not, on the environment

The Environment Agency (EA) is a non-departmental public body established in 1996 and sponsored by the Department for Environment, Food and Rural Affairs (DEFRA), with responsibilities relating to "the protection and enhancement" of the environment in England. It also, until 2013, had responsibility for Wales. It is not generally regarded as a regulator although it does regulate all sorts of activities, issuing licences for various activities and having fingers in many pies.

Established in 1996 the agency has its head office in Bristol, another office in London and further offices across England which is divided into 14 areas. It has close to 10,000 employees and in the year ended 31st March 2019 it spent around £1.06 billion, not far short of half of that on staff, with DEFRA providing most of the funding.

In the annual report for 2018-19, Emma Howard Boyd, who chairs the agency, wrote: "This report shows the Environment Agency is not only facing the world's climate emergency head on, it is unlocking opportunities for the economy as it goes," and concluded, "The decade between 2020 and 2030 will be crucial in terms of reducing emissions, increasing climate resilience, and avoiding ecological breakdown. The brilliant people of the Environment Agency are committed to making every single one of those ten years count."

"Our vision," the agency says, "is to create a better place for people and wildlife. We have three main business areas: flood and coastal erosion risk management; water, land and biodiversity; and regulated business."

It has, in fact, an extraordinarily wide remit, including boating (boat registration, conditions on the Thames and its bridges and locks, etc.); chemicals (including land contamination and monitoring emissions); climate change agreements (including setting them up and managing them); emissions and emissions trading; energy efficiency; environmental permits for such things as septic tanks and treatment plants; environmental planning – giving advice to developers, local planning authorities, transport authorities and agencies; fisheries and rod licensing, including permission to trap crayfish, eels, elvers, salmon and sea trout; land management, to prevent harmful weeds and invasive non-native plants spreading; harnessing hydroelectric power and also assessing designs for new nuclear power stations (in addition to its involvement in nuclear regulation and monitoring radioactivity); oil spills as well as oil storage regulations for businesses; registering waste carriers and assessing the disposal of business or commercial waste including hazardous waste; and so on … and on.

In its 2016-17 annual report, it said that its "aim is to always reduce the burden on businesses from regulation, so whenever we change the way we regulate, we assess the impact of this on businesses. This contributes to the government's overall business burden reduction target, known as the business impact target".

It also trumpeted that it was "an organisation continually striving to be the best, focused on outcomes and constantly challenging itself".

In Wales, much of what the Environment Agency does for England is carried out by Natural Resources Wales, a Welsh Government-sponsored body which became operational on 1st April 2013 when it took over the management of the natural resources of Wales. It was formed from a merger of the Countryside Council for Wales, Environment Agency Wales and the Forestry Commission Wales, and assumed some other roles formerly taken by the Welsh Assembly. Its stated purpose is to "look after our environment for people and nature".

Scotland has the Scottish Environment Protection Agency, a non-departmental public body of the Scottish Government, whose role is "to make sure that the environment and human health are protected, to ensure that Scotland's natural resources and services are used as sustainably as possible and contribute to sustainable economic growth". It employs about 1,300 people to "regulate and advise on a wide range of environmental activities".

Northern Ireland has the Northern Ireland Environment Agency "which works to protect, conserve and promote the natural environment and built heritage for the benefit of present and future generations" under the Northern Ireland Department of Agriculture, Environment and Rural Affairs.

It could, perhaps should, be asked why so much flooding continues to occur in many parts of the UK with such committed regulators in charge of the environment. The most basic tasks appear to be overlooked or ignored, despite the heartfelt pleas from those most affected. Why, in fact, are the regulators not doing what they have been set up to do? In general, floods neither protect nor enhance the environment!

'Upholding information rights', whatever that means

According to its website, the Information Commissioner's Office (ICO) "upholds information rights in the public interest, promoting openness by public bodies and data privacy for individuals". It is an executive non-departmental public body sponsored by the Department for Digital, Culture, Media & Sport (DCMS).

According to its annual reports, it has a "mission" – to uphold information rights for the UK public in the digital age; a "vision" – to increase the confidence that the UK public have in organisations that process personal data and those which are responsible for making public information available; and five "strategic goals" – (1) to increase the public's trust and confidence in how data is [sic] used and made available, (2) improve standards of information rights practice through clear, inspiring and targeted engagement and influence, (3) maintain and develop influence within the global information rights regulatory community, (4) stay relevant, provide excellent public service and keep abreast of evolving technology, and (5) enforce the laws we help shape and oversee.

The ICO has been given powers of regulation relating to a great deal of legislation, including: the Data Protection Act 2018 (which replaced the 1998

Act) and the General Data Protection Regulation (GDPR) which came into effect in May 2018; The Freedom of Information Act 2000; The Environmental Information Regulations 2004; The Privacy and Electronic Communications Regulations 2003; The Network and Information Systems Regulations 2018; The Infrastructure for Spatial Information in the European Community Regulations 2009 (known as INSPIRE); The Re-use of Public Sector Information Regulations 2015; The Investigatory Powers Act 2016; and The Electronic Identification and Trust Services for Electronic Regulations 2016. Quite a remit.

It has offices in Wilmslow, Cheshire – its head office – and other offices in London, Cardiff, Belfast and Edinburgh, with the last three carrying out, in the Information Commissioner's own words, "critical outreach work to citizens and organisations in those nations and regions of the UK".

In 2018-19, the ICO spent a total of £43.32 million (a rise of nearly £16 million on the previous year), £29.04 million of which was on its staff of around 640 (a whopping increase on 2017-18).

The ICO's data protection activities are financed by fees collected from data controllers who have to notify their processing of personal data under the Data Protection Act, which "controls how your personal information is used by organisations, businesses or the government". The annual fee is set in three tiers: the lowest tier of £40 applies to charities and small organisations with fewer than 250 employees but rises in tier 3 to as much as £2,900 for larger concerns. Fee income was close to £40 million in 2018-19, almost twice that achieved in the previous year.

One aspect of its work is tackling nuisance calls and unsolicited marketing, which is something you might have thought would fall to Ofcom.

For example, in 2015 the *Daily Mail* and *Mail on Sunday* made allegations about how some charities were misusing people's personal data. The allegations were about nuisance calls, breaches of the Privacy and Electronic Communications Regulations 2003 (PECR), and the widespread trading and sharing of donors' personal details.

Following investigations, the ICO found that some charities had shared personal data with third party organisations without telling the people concerned. The investigation resulted in the ICO issuing 13 civil monetary penalties to the value of £181,000. The Commissioner at the time exercised her discretion to set a reduced level of penalty that "would encourage better practice while not unduly distressing donors". In other words, the charities were given a light rap on the knuckles, showing the ICO's soft heart, while many of us continued to receive those inconvenient and jolly annoying calls.

In August 2017, the ICO reports, "benchmark research" showed that on average only one in five people in the UK public has trust and confidence in companies and organisations using their personal data.

"We want to improve this number in the years ahead," it says. "But, educating the entire UK public is a huge task."

To start on this "huge task", the ICO launched a "Your Data Matters" campaign in 2018, with "off the shelf" communications materials (including a poster where people's faces are comprised of fingerprints) available to organisations "who [sic] share this goal" and guidance for members of the public about their rights under the new data protection law.

"The campaign strapline, logo and communications material are the result of a close collaboration between the ICO and representatives from public and private sector organisations.

"The aim is to deliver consistent educational messages that will help individuals understand the changing data protection environment in a practical and straightforward way. Messages that organisations, regardless of their sector or size, can refer to, link to or repeat to complement their own customer and staff communications. We hope the campaign can ease the burden on organisations having to create their own materials while at the same time ensuring a coherent message is communicated."

The campaign has that wonderfully patronising approach that so many regulators adopt. The fact that the public lacks trust and confidence in companies and organisations which use their personal data should surely encourage the regulator to look at why this is the case and ensure that companies and organisations are better educated in data usage. The ICO might argue that it is doing just that, but with so many "data breaches" occurring it has clearly been failing. We can only wish them success with the campaign, but would urge them to at least use better grammar and rename it "Your data matter".

Keeping watch on surveillance cameras

The role of the Surveillance Camera Commissioner (SCC) is to encourage compliance with the surveillance camera code of practice. The office of the commissioner was created by the Home Office under the Protection of Freedoms Act 2012 "to further regulate CCTV", but the commissioner is described as "independent of government".

The Act required a code of practice to be produced about surveillance camera systems and set out new guidelines for CCTV and automatic number plate recognition.

The commissioner is required to encourage compliance with the surveillance camera code of practice, review how it is working and provide advice to ministers on whether or not the code needs amending.

The commissioner, oddly, has no enforcement or inspection powers but works with relevant authorities to make them aware of their duty "to have regard to the code". The code is not applicable to domestic use in private households. The commissioner must also consider how best to encourage voluntary adoption of the code by other operators of surveillance camera systems.

So, there is a code of practice which is not enforced by anyone but there is a commissioner who encourages voluntary compliance – which is hardly regulation!

What, then, does the SCC actually do? It has established an advisory council to give advice on specific areas relating to surveillance camera systems and has a standards group "to work on simplifying and improving the surveillance camera system standards framework".

Writing in the annual report for the year ended 31st March 2017, the commissioner said: "In the context of surveillance camera systems, good surveillance is best delivered by equipment that: conforms to industry standards, is situated in locations where it is justifiably most needed and will most benefit the public interest; is lawfully and transparently operated by competent authorities and individuals trained to accredited standards, with the privacy of the individual citizen at the heart of system and procedural decision making.

"The litmus test for good surveillance is of course a high degree of public confidence in the lawful and ethical use of surveillance camera systems in accordance with the Surveillance Camera Code of Practice (SC Code). Bad surveillance is conducted when these standards are absent, where the public lacks confidence in its presence and operation, and are confused about where accountability for its use and regulatory accountability lies.

"The privacy of individual citizens is a fundamental consideration of lawful governance of a surveillance camera system."

He continued: "It is a nonsense that the smallest of parish councils in England and Wales must have regard to the SC Code in the operation of their surveillance camera systems yet [referring to organisations such as Transport for London, the Highways Agency, rail franchises, airports and seaports, CCTV systems operated in crowded places and those cameras that cover the critical national infrastructure] the operators of such huge and intrusive systems that invade upon the everyday life of citizens, do not. I continue to lobby government for a more common sense position."

At one point he asks: "Why is data accuracy a concern?" His answer begins, "Data accuracy is a concern because accuracy and security of data are essential." You could hardly say anything fairer – or more tautologous – than that.

The SCC has called for automatic number plate recognition (ANPR) to receive "legislative oversight" and has urged the government to place it on a statutory footing. ANPR is described as one of the largest non-military databases in the UK with a national infrastructure of approximately 9,000 cameras that capture between 25 and 40 million pieces of data (citizens' number plates) per day and up to 20 billion "read" records are held.

In 2017, the Information Commissioner and the Surveillance Camera Commissioner issued a "memorandum of understanding" – a revision of an earlier one. They described the memorandum as a statement of intent that had at its heart the protection of the fundamental rights and freedoms of citizens in respect of their privacy, the protection of their personal information and also the public interest which arises when balancing those considerations against a legitimate duty to protect communities, where it is necessary to do so.

"It clearly sets out a framework for co-operation, co-ordination and information sharing between the Surveillance Camera Commissioner and the Information Commissioner in connection with the sharing of relevant information and the delivery of their statutory functions where it is considered by the commissioners to be in the public interest for them to do so."

Two bodies working together for the common good. How very reassuring.

You can bet that gambling is regulated – sort of

The Gambling Commission is an executive non-departmental public body sponsored by the Department for Digital, Culture, Media & Sport. It was set up under the Gambling Act 2005 to regulate commercial gambling in Great Britain in partnership with licensing authorities. Its strapline reads: "Making gambling fairer and safer."

In 2013 it assumed responsibility for regulating the National Lottery. It should be noted that the commission is not responsible for granting planning permission for bookmakers' shops – such decisions are made by local authorities in England, Scotland and Wales, and the regulation of spread betting is the responsibility of the Financial Conduct Authority.

The Gambling Commission is charged with regulating arcades, betting, bingo, casinos, gaming machine providers, gambling software providers, lottery operators, external lottery managers and remote gambling systems (online and by phone) that use British-based equipment, in England, Wales and Scotland. Northern Ireland has a different system, many years behind the times of the rest of the UK but is working hard to catch up.

The commission says that it "regulates the gambling industry in Great Britain, keeping gambling fair, safe and crime free by placing consumers at the heart of regulation, maintaining the integrity of the gambling industry and being an exemplar of best practice internationally".

The commission has about 300 employees, mostly based at its offices in Birmingham, with quite a few home-based staff working across England, Scotland and Wales. In 2018-19 expenditure was £27.58 million (nearly £7 million more than in the previous year); £17.46 million went on staff; £18.46 million came from licence fees, the rest from the government.

Among its stated objectives are to protect children and other vulnerable persons from being harmed or exploited by gambling; and to regulate the National Lottery "to ensure that every lottery that forms a part of it is run with all due propriety".

Part of the chairman's message in the 2016-17 annual report read: "The gambling industry provides entertainment that many people value and it creates jobs and wealth. However, problem gambling has a real cost to the economy and to the individuals and families affected by it, although the scale of the adverse impact is currently poorly understood. Public opinion also needs to be taken into account. Even those who are strong supporters of gambling share some of the concerns expressed by the wider public about the place of gambling in society."

He continued: "The proportion of people who believe that gamblers should be able to gamble whenever they want has dropped from 78% in 2010 to 67% in 2016." (Note that no margin of error was given for these figures which are likely to be as unreliable as the majority of polls in the UK and elsewhere.)

"Another important indicator of changing public opinion," he continued, "is the proportion of people who believe gambling is dangerous to family life. In 2010 this stood at 62% whereas by 2016 this had risen to 69%. Finally, the proportion of the population who believe that gambling should be discouraged has risen from 36% in 2010 to 55% in 2016.

"It would appear from these figures that public attitudes towards gambling have become less tolerant. This is a trend which we must recognise and will influence our approach to regulation."

He added that the scale of gambling-related harm was not at all clear and that definitions and estimates differed. "At the moment," he wrote, "we estimate that there are around 320,000 problem gamblers and a further 2.5 million are at risk of experiencing gambling harm."

He also wrote that: "Great Britain now has the largest regulated online gambling market in the world with around 21 million active accounts."

Other data given about the "gambling industry" reveal that in 2016 the total gross yield in Great Britain was £13.8 billion, with 106,678 people employed, 8,788 betting shops, 583 bingo premises, 147 casinos and 176,410 gaming machines. Contributions to "good causes" from the National Lottery from April 2016 to March 2017 were £1.6 billion, a 15% decrease on the previous year. Spending on the lottery in that year was £6.9 billion, down from £7.6 billion in 2015-16.

What we have seen in recent years is a huge increase in "gambling" advertising, with many ads being screened during television programmes or appearing in publications that children have ready access to; there has also been a proliferation of other lotteries, which may explain the drop in support for the National Lottery.

The ridiculous exhortations to "gamble responsibly" and "When the fun stops stop" were never likely to dampen the enthusiasm of addicts and the problems are only likely to get worse. Quite what "placing consumers at the heart of regulation" means will probably remain as great a mystery to the public and those being regulated as it is to the Gambling Commission.

Promoting 'responsible gambling standards'

The Senet Group describes itself as an independent body set up to "promote responsible gambling standards", supporting the Gambling Commission's work to make services safer and fairer, especially by ensuring that responsible gambling messages are communicated to players with frequency and prominence.

It was created by four of Britain's main gambling companies – William Hill, Ladbrokes, Coral and Paddy Power – in response to public concerns on gambling, and gambling advertising in particular. It also has a number of "funding partners" or "funding partnership relationships" with William Hill Organisation Ltd, Ladbrokes Coral PLC, Sky Betting and Gaming PLC, Paddy Power/Betfair PLC and Scotbet PLC.

It states that the content used in its media campaigns and player messaging activity reflects the findings of independent surveys "into the reach and effectiveness of our campaigns".

It issues "best practice guidance" on responsible gambling messaging and advertising and explains on its website not just how to contact the Senet Group itself but also other regulatory and charitable bodies, such as Gamblers Anonymous, with a role in preventing problem gambling.

Deciding what is or is not 'competitive'

Once upon a time, the UK had a Competition Commission but this was closed on 1st April 2014 (along with the Office of Fair Trading) and replaced by the Competition and Markets Authority (CMA).

In late 2013 the soon-to-be CMA published a document setting out its aims and ambitions. The CMA, it read, has: a *primary duty* – "to seek to promote competition, both within and outside the United Kingdom, for the benefit of consumers"; a *mission* – "to make markets work well in the interests of consumers, businesses and the economy"; and an *overall ambition* – "to consistently be one of the leading competition and consumer agencies in the world". Don't you love it when an organisation has such detailed yet woolly goals?

One of its numerous stated goals is to "complement the work of other consumer, regulatory and enforcement authorities, and act as a trusted competition adviser across government" and it says that if it has success with its goals it will be "an authority that has a beneficial impact on consumers, on business behaviour and on productivity and growth in the economy"; a respected and influential independent authority in the UK and abroad; and a great place to work.

The CMA is described as "an independent non-ministerial department" and a "unitary authority". At the end of March 2019 it employed just over 850 people, working mainly at its London office along with representatives in Scotland, Wales and Northern Ireland. Staff costs totalled £53.35 million.

In 2018-19 the authority spent £98.9 million, £65 million on what it called "our business as usual activities of protecting consumers through effective enforcement, operating an effective and efficient merger regime, making markets work better, being a strong voice for competition, and strong partnerships".

Another £24.6 million was spent on construction work and fitting out the office space for its move into plush new London headquarters at Canary Wharf. The CMA team in Edinburgh has also got new offices. Says the CMA: "As part of these moves we expect to increase productivity, reduce costs, improve wellbeing, support the attraction and retention of top talent and contribute to wider objectives including sustainability." Who could possibly begrudge such spending knowing it will produce such splendid results?

It also spent £7.7 million on preparations for the CMA's expanded role after the UK exits the EU, which includes developing a new "state aid function". It stated: "The UK's exit from the EU (Exit) presents opportunities for the CMA to secure better outcomes for UK consumers by taking a bigger role on the world stage post-Exit." Make of that what you will. But it will provide employment for more than 450 people at the CMA.

The CMA has set up a "forum" called The UK Competition Network (UKCN) with all UK regulators that have a specific role in supporting and enabling competition within their sectors. The CMA says the network aims to encourage stronger competition for the benefit of consumers and to prevent anti-competitive behaviour in the regulated industries. One would have thought the latter aim was a principal role of regulators such as Ofgem and Ofcom, but apparently they need help from the CMA in doing the jobs they should already be doing.

In its annual report for 2016-17, the CMA said: "We're tackling problems which mean that customers are paying £1.4 billion each year more than they would in a fully competitive energy market. And we've stepped in to protect pre-payment meter customers with a temporary price cap, saving them £300 million pa." Again, one might wonder what Ofgem had been doing and why it had not dealt with these matters.

This raises the issue of "concurrency", which means two regulators doing the same job, although the CMA expresses it differently. It says that concurrency "refers to the fact that both the CMA and sector regulators (such as the regulators in the communications, energy, water, aviation, rail, healthcare, financial services and payment systems sectors) have powers to enforce the prohibitions against anti-competitive agreements and abuses of a dominant position in the regulated sectors and can also carry out market studies and refer markets to the CMA for a detailed investigation".

The CMA produces an annual report on concurrency, telling us in the one published in April 2018 that: "Competition in the regulated sectors is particularly important, as almost every household and business in the UK relies on their services; from basic utilities like heat, light and water to financial services such as banking and insurance. These sectors are also estimated to represent around 25% of GDP.

"It's important to have a concurrency regime that works well," it continues. "This is to ensure that the benefits that competition can bring to us all – including bringing prices down, and increasing quality standards – are secured in the regulated sectors. The government recognised this importance and developed an enhanced concurrency regime which came into effect in 2014 as part of the reforms to the UK's competition regime. It introduced several mechanisms to facilitate greater and more effective use of competition powers in the regulated sectors, to create a system of case allocation between the CMA and the regulators, and to encourage closer co-operation."

"So, how well have things been working?" the CMA asks. It answers its own question by saying that almost every regulator has now launched at least one Competition Act (CA98) investigation; the CMA and the regulators have also undertaken significant markets work; the regulators and the CMA have developed strong relationships, regularly sharing best practice on both substantive and procedural issues in competition cases; regular secondments take place between CMA staff and the regulators, effectively sharing resources and expertise; co-operation extends beyond concurrent CA98 and markets work to other policy projects promoting competition in the regulated sectors, as well as remedies work and mergers.

The CMA also notes: "We are very pleased with the progress we have made since the new concurrency arrangements came into effect, and particularly the noticeable step change in the relationships that have developed between the CMA and the regulators."

Which can give us all a warm feeling that all these regulators are acting in our best interests.

Trying to see that everyone trades 'properly'

National Trading Standards was set up in 2012 by the government as part of changes "to the consumer protection landscape". Its stated role is to provide leadership, influence, support and resources to help combat consumer and business detriment nationally, regionally and locally, bringing together trading standards representatives from England and Wales to prioritise, fund and co-ordinate national and regional enforcement cases.

Its vision is "to protect consumers and safeguard businesses through cross-boundary intelligence-led enforcement projects in England and Wales. By looking beyond local boundaries, we aim to monitor, disrupt and bring to justice individuals and organised crime groups committing trading standards offences".

The body is governed by a board that has an "independent" chairperson and 10 representatives from the regional trading standards groups in England and Wales.

Funding is provided by the Department of Business Innovation and Skills (BIS) – £13.46 million in 2018-19; the Home Office – £700,000 for knife crime and scams; plus another £2.7 million from other sources for particular projects.

It has various teams operating, including an eCrime Team, Estate Agency Team, Illegal Money Lending Teams, Intelligence Team, Safety at Ports and Borders Teams, Regional Investigations Teams, Scams Team, and a Feed Hygiene Delivery Team, and it also works with the Advertising Standards Authority.

Northern Ireland and Scotland have their own services: the role of Northern Ireland Trading Standards Service is "to promote and maintain fair trading, protect consumers and help reputable businesses to thrive within Northern Ireland"; while Trading Standards Scotland looks after such matters in that part of the UK. The latter is funded by the BIS and managed by the Convention of Scottish Local Authorities (COSLA), the representative body of local government in Scotland.

In addition there is a Chartered Trading Standards Institute, a not-for-profit membership organisation founded in 1881 which is not a "regulator" but an organisation which exists to represent trading standards professionals working in the UK and overseas – in local authorities, business and consumer sectors and central government. It received a Royal Charter in 2015.

It aims, it says, "to promote and protect the success of a modern vibrant economy, and safeguard the health, safety and wellbeing of citizens by enhancing the professionalism of its members", and one of its "key messages" is: "We are consumer protection experts and will continue to work with governments and our partners to deliver our vision for larger, more strategic and sustainable trading standards services."

Again, make of that what you will.

Working to ensure charities are charitable

The job of the Charity Commission is to register and regulate charities in England and Wales, in order to "ensure that the public can support charities with confidence".

It is an independent (that word yet again), non-ministerial government department accountable to parliament. It employs 400 people and has four offices – in London, Liverpool, Newport and Taunton. Net operating expenditure in the financial year ended 31st March 2017 was £22.9 million, of which close to £15.9 million went on staff costs. In 2018-19 its budget was £27.1 million, funded largely by a grant from the Treasury of £25.5 million.

The highest earner at the commission received a fairly charitable £130,000-plus in 2018-19, while the median remuneration of staff was a mere £28,649 – that figure being down by nearly £2,000 on the previous year.

The commission is responsible for maintaining an accurate and up-to-date register of charities: this includes deciding whether organisations are charitable and should be registered. It removes charities from its register that are not considered to be charitable, no longer exist or do not operate.

At 31st March 2017 there were 167,063 charities (and 16,455 subsidiaries) on the register and in the financial year which ended that day the commission "regulated" £74.7 billion of charity income, almost £4 billion more than the previous year, and over £71 billion of charity spend.

Among the decisions it took that year was that the Countryside Alliance, which had applied to register as a charity, could not be so registered, as some of the purposes of the organisation were not charitable for the public benefit. The Theosophical Society in England was, however, accepted for registration. Its purposes are to promote moral and spiritual welfare and the advancement of education through the promotion and study of Theosophy. In 1943 and 1957, the High Court decided that Theosophy was not a religion for the purposes of charity law, and the commission considered whether changes in the law since those decisions meant that the organisation could now be registered as a charity; it concluded that the purposes of this organisation are exclusively charitable purposes for the public benefit. Really?

The Commission has a range of statutory powers that it can use to stop abuse and to protect charitable assets and beneficiaries, including restricting the transactions that a charity may enter into, appointing additional trustees or freezing a charity's bank account.

In 2017, the commission registered a new type of charity: the first Charitable Authorised Investment Fund (CAIF). This is a form of collective investment scheme which is authorised by the Financial Conduct Authority. Although charitable collective investment arrangements were already available, in the form of common investment funds (CIFs), CAIFs are said to offer the advantages of FCA authorisation and regulation and the ability to operate as a unit trust. The charities investment market is a substantial one: the top 10 investment firms serving the market manage £32 billion of assets for nearly 1,600 charities. This is apparently a tax-efficient way for charities to invest their money – presumably for "the public benefit".

Each CAIF is to have "dual regulation" – by the FCA and the Charity Commission. The Charity Commission is responsible for registration of the CAIF as a charity and regulates the CAIF (and the charity trustees) in respect of compliance with charity law. The FCA is responsible for authorising the CAIF as an authorised fund and regulates the operation and administration of the CAIF and its compliance with the financial services law and regulation including the FCA rules. The two regulators say they have agreed arrangements to ensure their respective roles are clear and that regulation and supervision of CAIFs operate as intended.

There are, it should be said, charitable trusts which like to (in some cases are required to) keep their capital intact and so invest it and make grants, etc., from the income, so we mustn't be too critical.

In other cases, however, it might interest people who donate funds to charities to know that vast sums are being stored up in this way rather than being used for the purposes for which they thought they were being given – generally for helping people and/or animals – rather than making money for investment companies. But no doubt there are good reasons for it and the Charity Commission can justify it "for the public benefit".

In Scotland, charities are registered and regulated by the Scottish Charity Regulator (another independent body) – 24,416 were registered by March 2018, including community groups, religious charities, schools, universities, grant-giving charities and major care providers.

The following were registered as charities during March 2018: 117th City of Edinburgh Brownie Unit; 11th Bearsden Brownie Unit; 137th City of Edinburgh Rainbow Unit; 1st Bonkle Guide Unit; 1st Muchalls and Newtonhill Brownie Unit; 4th Peterhead Brownie Unit; 50th City of Dundee Guide Unit; Abbie's Sparkle Foundation; Advocacy Shetland; Arab Referentiality; ArtSquat; Balmaclellan Village Hall; Billboard Junction; Bonnymuir Green Community Trust; Bonnyton Community Association;

Bowmore Primary School Parent Council; Broch Community First Responders; Butterfly Day Centre; and Carnoustie High School Former Pupils' Rugby Football Club. Quite a busy month for the regulator.

It is officially estimated that the charity sector in Scotland handles more than £10 billion a year and that 183,000 people in Scotland are charity trustees – with many more as volunteers, paid staff and beneficiaries.

The Charity Commission for Northern Ireland was established under the Charities Act (Northern Ireland) 2008 and amended in 2013. It is, in its own words, "the independent regulator of charities in Northern Ireland, responsible for ensuring Northern Ireland has a dynamic and well-governed charities sector in which the public can have confidence". It is a non-departmental public body and is sponsored by the Department for Communities.

As of 31st March 2017, there were just over 5,500 charities on the register of charities – an increase of 1,500 in 12 months. Commission spending was a little under £2 million with £1.33 million spent on staff.

Overseeing the way we are persuaded to vote

The Electoral Commission is described as "the independent body which oversees elections and regulates political finance in the UK" and it says, "We work to promote public confidence in the democratic process and ensure its integrity."

It is divided into four main directorates: Communications and Research, Electoral Administration and Guidance, Finance and Corporate Services, and Political Finance and Regulation; and is led by nine commissioners who agree the working strategy and set the priorities for the executive team of chief executive, director of electoral administration and guidance, director of political finance and regulation and legal counsel, director of communications and research and director of finance and corporate services. Then there is a senior leadership group for all four directorates, plus a considerable number of committees, including: Speaker's Committee, Audit Committee, Remuneration and HR Committee, Parliamentary Advisory Group, Parliamentary Parties Panel, Northern Ireland Assembly Parties Panel, Scottish Parliament Political Parties Panel and Wales Assembly Parties Panel.

The commission's principal stated objectives are: well-run elections, referendums [should that not be referenda?] and electoral registration; transparency in party and election finance, with high levels of compliance.

It says: "We work to support well-run elections and referendums in the UK, offering support and guidance to those involved. We also work to ensure voters know everything they need to know about the process of casting their vote.

"As regulator of political party finances, we work to make sure people understand the rules around political party finance. Alongside this work, we also take action when the rules are broken and publish information on political finance."

In addition, the Commission maintains and publishes the registers of political parties in Great Britain and Northern Ireland: a political party has to be registered with the Commission in order to field candidates at an election; and it conducts a wide range of research around elections and referendums, electoral registration and party and election finance – to "ensure that our views and recommendations are evidence-based".

Finally, the Commission "runs campaigns before elections and referendums to make sure people are aware of when and how to register to vote and anything else they need to know".

The Commission spent £144.25 million in the 2016-17 financial year (less than it had been allowed to) and had average staff numbers of 132 full-time equivalents in offices in London, Cardiff, Edinburgh and Belfast. Its financial statements are just about the least intelligible of any regulator currently operating in the UK – but the Comptroller and Auditor General and the Treasury are happy with them.

Political party finance and the financing of campaigns is one of the thorniest problems facing the Commission, which acts, if it acts at all, retrospectively over breaches of its rules by parties or candidates or, in the case of the EU referendum of 2016, by groups leading the "Leave" or "Remain" campaigns. One group on the Leave side (Leave.EU) was fined £70,000 for a breach, but not until nearly two years after the referendum.

It was reported (though not by the Electoral Commission) that one donor, businessman Aaron Banks who was co-founder of the Leave.EU campaign and had previously made substantial donations to the Conservative Party, donated £12 million "of services" to the campaign led by Nigel Farage to leave the EU – making him the biggest donor to a political campaign in UK history. Amazing that one man can use such financial muscle to achieve what he personally wants!

The whole issue of election and referendum funding stinks and while there are discussions from time to time on changing the way things are done, nothing actually happens. Relatively small numbers of people, or companies, give vast sums to fund the party they wish to support and parties – particularly the Conservatives, although Labour and the Liberal Democrats are also affected – are given money by all sorts of people wishing to exert influence over them. The wealthy can buy access for meetings with cabinet ministers and the money goes into party funds. Prime ministers and leading politicians and party members prostrate themselves before potential donors, no matter how shady they are.

Just occasionally a party is shamed into returning money given by someone seeking to exert undue influence over it; although more often, donors end up complaining that the party they have given substantial money to is not doing what they would like it to!

Political funding came under particular scrutiny in the early part of this century as it became clear that the bigger political parties were highly dependent on a handful of wealthy donors – some of whom were apparently expecting honours, such as peerages, in return, and sometimes getting them. Numerous enquiries followed, making all sorts of recommendations, such as capping individual donations at £50,000 (from the 2006 enquiry) and then £10,000 (from the 2011 enquiry) – but, of course, nothing changed, other than the fact that more money was allocated by parliament for, essentially, administrative costs incurred by political parties.

Individual candidates in wards or constituencies are severely restricted in the amount of money they can spend to get themselves elected, but at national level parties are free to spend pretty much whatever they can raise. There is often confusion between national and local spending but the Electoral Commission explains this in an "expert paper" for election agents: "Party and candidate spending are sometimes referred to as 'local' and 'national' spending, but it is better to think of 'party' and 'candidate' spending. Not all local spending is automatically candidate spending – it is possible for party spending to occur at a local level. Because party spending is defined as any campaign spending other than candidate spending, you should always consider first whether any spending is candidate spending." Which clears that up, I'm sure you'll agree.

At some elections there are different spending limits for different parts of the UK. Spending at national level on the 2017 general election totalled £39.15 million, according to figures published by the Electoral Commission; just over £31 million was spent on "market research/canvassing", £13.4 million on sending unsolicited material to electors; and just over £10 million on advertising. But the stench surrounding the funding of the political parties remains. It has been described by some as a threat to "our democracy" and it is hard to argue with that.

'Ensuring the quality' of health and social care services

The Care Quality Commission (CQC) is "the independent regulator of health and social care in England". It is an executive non-departmental public body, sponsored by the Department of Health and Social Care, and its remit is to monitor, inspect and regulate health and social care services in England.

It was set up in 2009 to replace three existing bodies: the Healthcare Commission, the Commission for Social Care Inspection and the Mental Health Act Commission.

According to the government website, the commission "ensures the quality and safety of care in hospitals, dentists, ambulances, and care homes, and the care given in people's own homes". Given the condition of the healthcare sector, "ensures" might be too strong a word; "looks at" would be a better term, as it would be more in tune with reality.

According to the CQC's own website, the way it regulates care services involves: "registering people that apply to us to provide services; using data, evidence and information throughout our work; using feedback you've given us to help us reach our judgements; inspections carried out by experts; publishing information on our judgements – in most cases we also publish a rating to help you choose care; taking action when we judge that services need to improve or to make sure those responsible for poor care are held accountable for it."

In its 2016-17 annual report, the chairman and chief executive, in a joint statement, noted: "We are the only country in the world to have an independent assessment of the quality of health and social care by a single regulator."

Further on in the annual report there was a comment on "enforcement action", which read: "When we find poor care, we act quickly and effectively to protect people. We took more enforcement action this year than last year (1,910 compared with 1,090 actions) and, since receiving new powers to prosecute in April 2015, we strengthened the capacity of our staff and improved our enforcement recording processes. We also took our first enforcement action against two online providers of primary care, protecting the public regardless of how they access care. When we find serious failings in care, we recommend that providers are put in special measures – 740 providers were placed in special measures and 657 exited special measures. Of those that exited, 470 did so because they had made substantial improvement."

The CQC employed more than 3,200 people in 2016-17, at a cost of more than £171 million. It collected nearly £150 million in "regulatory fees for chargeable activities" but spent over £197 million on these activities (including the staff costs); total expenditure for the year was £235.65 million. Grant-in-aid from the Department of Health was £81.7 million. Two years later its income was up to more than £205 million and it spent over £238 million, nearly £174 million of that on staff.

The CQC's early years were marked by controversy and well-merited accusations of severe failings. In December 2015 Parliament's Public Accounts Committee was highly critical of the CQC, noting that reports prepared by the regulator contained numerous errors; one foundation trust said that its staff had found more than 200 errors in a draft report.

In July 2016 the commission issued an apology after admitting that up to 500 Disclosure and Barring Service certificates submitted by applicants to become registered managers and providers had been lost during a planned office refurbishment: a locked filing cabinet had been incorrectly marked up to be taken away and destroyed.

Intriguingly, the lady who chaired the CQC for its first four years had also been chief executive of the NHS West Midlands Strategic Health Authority: she had been responsible for supervising the performance of the hospital in Stafford where poor care had led to hundreds of avoidable or premature deaths between 2005 and 2008.

It's fascinating to see how people in top positions in the NHS who make a hash of their job get a substantial payout to leave and then, lo and behold, move into another similar, highly-paid position within the NHS or take a senior position with a regulator in pretty quick time.

Anyhow, after considerable changes in personnel, especially at the top, and a right-good bollocking from almost everyone, the CQC began to get its act together, providing some proper regulatory oversight and doing what it should have been doing all along. It wasn't entirely successful in its efforts, however, being criticised severely at fairly regular intervals for failing to ensure the safety and well-being of mental health patients, in particular, in a number of institutions and only showing genuine concern after people (whistleblowers) had spoken out or television programmes such as the BBC's *Panorama* had highlighted shortcomings.

The CQC, however, covers just England. Wales has the Healthcare Inspectorate Wales, "the independent inspectorate and regulator of healthcare in Wales" which regulates and inspects NHS services and independent healthcare providers in Wales against a range of standards, policies, guidance and regulations to highlight areas requiring improvement; as well as the Care and Social Services Inspectorate Wales which regulates social care, early years services and Local Authority care support services.

Scotland has Healthcare Improvement Scotland which includes the Healthcare Environment Inspectorate, with its focus on reducing healthcare-associated infection risk to hospital patients, improving the care of elderly patients, and regulating independent healthcare services through an inspection framework.

Scotland also has the Care Inspectorate, the abbreviated name of the Social Care and Social Work Improvement Scotland, which scrutinises social care, social work and child protection services; it also has the Mental Welfare Commission for Scotland, which is said to promote the welfare of individuals with mental illness, learning disability or related conditions and investigates cases where it appears that there may be ill-treatment, deficiency in care and treatment or improper detention of any such person.

Northern Ireland has the Regulation and Quality Improvement Authority (RQIA) which registers and inspects a wide range of health and social care services, including nursing, residential care and children's homes, and is also responsible for the regulation of day care settings, domiciliary care agencies, nursing agencies and a range of independent healthcare services. The RQIA also has a role in assuring the quality of services provided by the Health and Social Care (HSC) Board, HSC trusts and agencies, to ensure that every aspect of care reaches the standards laid down by the Department of Health and expected by the public; and under the Health and Social Care (Reform) Act (NI) 2009, RQIA has a range of responsibilities for people with a mental illness and those with a learning disability, including preventing ill treatment, remedying any deficiency in care or treatment, terminating improper detention in a hospital or guardianship, and preventing or redressing loss or damage to a patient's property.

Care of the elderly, especially in nursing or care homes, is one area of great concern across all four countries. There are constant charges of mistreatment and even brutal care in such homes. Not one of the countries – or the regulators – has got to grips with the problem and all have failed miserably in their stated aims, England's CQC by the greatest amount.

The regulators may be independent but clearly they need firmer oversight.

Aiming to 'improve' health services

NHS Improvement (NHSI) is the quaintly-named body set up in 2016 as the sector regulator for health services in England. It is the operational name for an organisation that brought together "Monitor", "NHS Trust Development Authority", "Patient Safety" including the "National Reporting and Learning System", "Advancing Change Team" and "Intensive Support Teams". Monitor and the NHS Trust Development Authority still exist as legal entities and produce their own annual reports but are part of NHSI.

The resulting organisation says: "We build on the best of what these organisations did, but with a change of emphasis. Our priority is to offer support to providers and local health systems to help them improve."

It is responsible for overseeing foundation trusts and NHS trusts, as well as independent providers of NHS-funded care: "We offer the support these providers need to give patients consistently safe, high quality, compassionate care within local health systems that are financially sustainable. By holding providers to account and, where necessary, intervening, we help the NHS to meet its short-term challenges and secure its future."

According to its website, this body is "committed to working closely with the Care Quality Commission (CQC), NHS England and other partners, including professional regulators, at national, regional and local levels. We recognise that providers are frustrated by the fragmentation of national system-level organisations and the inconsistencies and extra burdens this brings.

"We will: collaborate with other arm's-length body colleagues to streamline the data requests made of providers and reduce the burden of regulation across the board; ensure a shared definition of quality and efficiency with CQC, and undertake the new use of resources assessment on CQC's behalf; work with NHS England to ensure greater alignment between the financial levers for commissioners and providers; and align with CQC and NHS England to create a single and simple definition of success for providers."

In its first year of operation NHSI employed about 550 people at a cost of £49.42 million out of a total spend of £76.74 million. It has a 12-member board, including five non-executive directors, an associate non-executive director and a senior independent director; and a 12-strong executive team which includes the chief executive (also a board member); a deputy chief executive who is also executive director of regulation; an executive medical director and chief operating officer; an executive director of nursing (also a board member); an executive director of improvement; four executive regional managing directors (for the north, Midlands and east, London, and south-east); an executive director of strategy; an executive director of operational productivity; and a chief financial officer.

All very impressive, it must be admitted.

In the other parts of the UK, Healthcare Improvement Scotland has as its purpose, "better quality health and social care for everyone in Scotland", and its work includes the regulation of independent hospitals and clinics; 1000 Lives Improvement is the national improvement service for NHS Wales delivered by Public Health Wales, with the aim of supporting the NHS to improve outcomes for people using services in Wales. Northern Ireland has no equivalent body but a variety of organisations do similar jobs.

"Improvements" everywhere, it would appear but so far more in theory than in practice.

Taking care of our civil airspace

The Civil Aviation Authority (CAA) is responsible for the regulation of aviation safety in the UK, determining policy for the use of airspace, the economic regulation of Heathrow, Gatwick and Stansted airports, the licensing and financial fitness of airlines and the management of the ATOL financial protection scheme for holidaymakers.

It is a public corporation of the Department for Transport, established by parliament in 1972 as an independent specialist aviation regulator. The government requires that its costs are met entirely from charges to those it provides a service to or regulates.

"The interests of the public and consumers are at the heart of all that we do," the CAA (in common with most regulators) proudly states. "We drive to be a transparent, fair and effective regulator, which is reflected in our recent work to streamline our processes, identify and remove regulatory burdens and become more risk-focussed. We are keen to ensure that our policy proposals are prepared to take account of the value, costs and benefits of alternative options for all stakeholders.

"While keeping the public and consumers at the forefront of our work, we must also balance these interests with creating a regulatory environment which supports growth in the aviation sector and avoids imposing unnecessary burdens on the industry."

A blog in April 2016 written by its "transformation programme manager" (there's a title) said: "Our aim is that by 2020 we will be a CAA ambitious for what it can achieve, focusing on the things that matter most, clear and proportionate in our regulation, and with modern processes and systems. And we will contribute to a world where everyone who chooses to fly, as well as those who do not, has confidence in a safe and secure aviation sector that takes its responsibilities seriously."

In the year ended 31st March 2017, the authority had income of £135.82 million, with £76.2 million spent on employment costs, and an operating profit of just under £5 million. The average number of staff during the year was 964, up from 927 the previous year. It does a great job in ensuring the safety of the nation's air space, setting the bar way above global (including the USA) standards. Top marks for that aspect of its work.

Writing in the 2016-17 annual report, the "chair" of the CAA said the authority was delighted that the government had decided that a new runway should be built in the south-east. She continued: "The third runway at Heathrow will be the biggest privately funded infrastructure project in the world. We are already working on the economic regulatory regime to achieve the right balance between shareholders' ability to finance the scheme and affordability for the airlines and their passengers.

"To do this we will work closely with the airport and the airlines. We are already doing significant preparatory work, and have set up a Consumer Challenge Board chaired by Jeff Halliwell who is the Chair of Transport Focus*, Airport Coordination Ltd (ACL)** and Anglian Water's Consumer Challenge Group. This group will scrutinise Heathrow's plans and advise us on whether consumers' needs are reflected in the airport's business plans and operations, and how well it is engaging with them. I have every confidence that it will do an excellent job of assessing the proposals and holding Heathrow to account."

That's a level of confidence that will not be shared by everyone.

* Transport Focus, an executive non-departmental public body sponsored by the Department for Transport, was previously Passenger Focus and had other names going back to 1947 when it was principally concerned with trains; in 2008 its remit was extended to buses and trams and in 2014 the Department for Transport widened its role further, from representing passengers to representing all those who use the motorways and certain A roads in England (the Strategic Road Network), including motorists, freight and business users, as well as those who walk or cycle on the network. It is officially the "road user watchdog".

** Airport Coordination Ltd is responsible for "slot allocation, schedules facilitation and schedule data collection" at nearly 40 airports around the world and also provides a wide range of services to the aviation industry. It has its head office at Heathrow and other offices in Manchester, Dubai and Auckland.

Holding the nuclear industry to account

The Office for Nuclear Regulation (ONR) is responsible for regulation of nuclear safety and security across the UK. Its mission, it says, is to provide efficient and effective regulation of the nuclear industry, holding it to account on behalf of the public.

As an "independent statutory corporation", it reports, oddly enough, to the Department for Work and Pensions (which doesn't cover Northern Ireland), although it also works closely with the Department of Energy and Climate Change.

According to its website, "ONR independently regulates nuclear safety and security at 36 nuclear licensed sites in the UK. We also regulate transport and ensure that safeguards obligations for the UK are met. Our duty is to ensure that the nuclear industry controls its hazards effectively, has a culture of continuous improvement and maintains high standards.

"The nuclear industry is undergoing rapid change and our role as a regulator is vital in ensuring new nuclear facilities are designed, built and operated to the highest standards, and in a manner that improves public confidence without compromising safety or security.

"We also oversee the decommissioning of nuclear sites and co-operate with international regulators on safety and security issues of common concern, including associated research.

"Our work is critical to the protection of society at large so it is important that we do it with rigour, diligence and with an appropriate level of assurance."

With a wonderful mangling of the English language, it goes on to say: "Before ONR can permission key activities, we assess licensees' safety cases, on a sample basis according to potential consequences, to ensure that the hazards have been understood and are properly controlled."

The regulator is made up of site inspectors and specialist inspectors, drawn from various professional fields including civil engineering, radiological protection, human factors, chemical engineering, mechanical engineering and nuclear physics.

The ONR states, "The inspectors are supported up by a business support team, which ensures that the programme functions effectively and efficiently, ensuring that the necessary administration and legal considerations are in order, handling enquiries from members of the public and other parties, and maintaining the lines of communication between inspectors and licensees.

"Every licensed site has a nominated site inspector who is ONR's primary point of contact for that site. The inspector typically spends around one week in four at the site, conducts routine site inspection for compliance with licence conditions, follows up incidents and events at the site. The inspector liaises with the licensee's personnel giving advice on how to comply with legal requirements, assessing the adequacy of safety cases and most importantly ensuring that risks to workers and members of the public are reduced so far as is reasonably practicable."

In its 2018-19 financial year the ONR had well over 500 staff, costing just under £52 million out of a total spend of £76.15 million, up from £64.5 million. Nearly £69 million of its income came from fees for the licensing of nuclear installations and contracts with "customers".

And it's all so we can rest easily in our beds.

'Assuring value' of some defence spending

SSRO (Single Source Regulations Office), which was set up in 2014, is described as "an executive non-departmental public body, sponsored by the Ministry of Defence" and "the independent statutory regulator of single source defence procurement", which operates under the slogan, "Assuring value, building confidence."

Its remit is to regulate the UK government's procurement of "single source" or non-competitive military goods, works and services. Its principal statutory aims are to ensure that good value for money is obtained for the UK taxpayer in expenditure on qualifying defence contracts, and that single source suppliers are paid a fair and reasonable price under those contracts.

In 2018-19 it had about 40 staff (a steadily rising number) at a cost of a little over £4.2 million, out of total expenditure of £6.12 million. As one of the newest regulators, it's starting relatively small but gradually expanding in both numbers and spending and now has its place on the UKRN (*see below*).

What is needed now, without doubt, is a body to regulate the Ministry of Defence itself and to look at the areas where the truly enormous cost overruns happen, such as with new warships and fighter aircraft.

Trying to make sure that supermarkets behave themselves

The Groceries Code Adjudicator (GCA) is, says the government, "the independent regulator ensuring that the 10 large supermarkets treat their direct suppliers lawfully and fairly". The GCA works with the Department for Business, Energy & Industrial Strategy and is designated as a "corporation sole".

The government introduced the GCA in 2013 with the job of "enforcing better treatment of UK supermarket suppliers". This followed an investigation in 2008 by the Competition Commission into supermarket supply chain relations.

The adjudicator has powers to launch investigations and hand out fines to retailers; and can receive complaints and arbitrate disputes between food suppliers and the UK's supermarket chains with a turnover in excess of £1 billion, of which there were 10 in 2013.

Retailers found by the adjudicator to be breaking the Groceries Supply Code – which covers buyer abuses, such as arbitrary retrospective changes to supply agreements and payment delays – can be compelled to publish apologies or receive fines. Complaints are limited to direct suppliers of supermarkets and not the entire supply chain, a restriction which disappointed the National Farmers' Union which wanted the adjudicator to cover it all.

In its annual report and accounts for the year ended 31st March 2018, a document running to more than 90 A4 pages, the GCA revealed that it had been appointed as arbitrator on two issues, launched one investigation (the second in its history), applied no enforcement measures, and made no recommendations to the Competitions and Markets Authority for changes to the code; however, it did commission a survey and held a conference in London attended by 250 people. Such a busy year!

In spite of this, expenditure in the year was £697,302, up from £622,024 in 2016-17, the increase reflecting, it says, additional costs incurred for awareness-raising and other activities. Staff costs were £450,156, compared to £415,483 the previous year.

Funding comes from a levy on the regulated retailers, plus recovery of costs of arbitrations undertaken, and of those investigations where one or more retailers are found to have breached the Groceries Supply Code.

According to newspaper reports in June 2018, more retailers were in line to be added to the GCA's remit. These included companies such as Amazon and

Boots, though quite how they would be fitted in was not apparent. The GCA said at the time that bringing these retailers up to speed and ensuring a consistent level of compliance would be challenging and exciting work. It certainly would be.

'An appropriate regime'
for forensic science services

The Forensic Science Regulator (we hadn't heard of it either) exists to ensure that the provision of forensic science services across the criminal justice system is subject to an appropriate regime of scientific quality standards.

Although sponsored by the Home Office, the regulator is "a public appointee" and operates independently of the Home Office on behalf of the criminal justice system as a whole. "This independence," it says, "allows us to make unbiased recommendations and decisions."

It collaborates with the authorities in Scotland and Northern Ireland who have expressed their willingness to be partners in the setting of quality standards which will be adopted within their justice systems.

The regulator is supported by a team of civil servants (three scientists) with additional support provided by shared services from the Home Office and Home Office Science Secretariat.

There are quite a number of working groups and sub-committees, including: Forensic Science Advisory Council; Contamination specialist group; Fingerprint quality specialist group; Digital forensics specialist group; DNA analysis specialist group; End user specialist group; Forensic pathology specialist group; Medical forensics specialist group; Quality standards specialist group; and Evidence assessment specialist group.

The annual report for the year ending in November 2017 showed that the regulator was allocated £524,684, a small reduction on the previous year, with £374,684 spent on staff pay, travel and accommodation, etc.

If there were to be an award for the most efficient regulator, the one which does considerable amounts of work while spending very little money, then it should, without doubt, go to this splendid outfit.

Some of the regulators link up

"Bringing regulators together for the benefit of consumers and the economy," proclaims the UK Regulators Network (UKRN), which was set up in 2014 by several of the main regulatory bodies in the UK to, in its own words, "provide the structure for regulators to consider common issues and policy projects with relevance across utility, financial and transport sectors".

A statement on its website says: "Since our formation, we have developed strong relationships with each other and encouraged a culture of collaboration and learning, which combines our strengths and facilitates the delivery of our statutory duties to the benefit of consumers and the economy.

"We regularly facilitate events and discussions of topical issues with external audiences and in collaboration with partners. In the past, these topics have included consumer policy, investment, innovation, infrastructure and the role of independent regulation.

"On occasions, we partner with appropriate organisations and think tanks to organise joint seminars and roundtables, which boosts our ability to reach different recipients and beneficiaries."

The members in October 2019 were: The Civil Aviation Authority (CAA); The Financial Conduct Authority (FCA); The Financial Reporting Council (FRC) – due to become the Audit, Reporting and Governance Authority in 2020; The Payment Systems Regulator (PSR); Office of Communications (Ofcom); Office of Gas and Electricity Markets (Ofgem); Water Services Regulation Authority (OfWat); Office of Rail and Road (ORR); Single Source Regulations Office (SSRO); Northern Ireland Authority for Utility Regulation; Legal Services Board (LSB); the Pensions Regulator; and the Information Commissioners Office. Water Industry Commission for Scotland (WICS) was a member in 2018 but not on the list when this was written.

The people who run the UKRN are seconded from member regulators and include, among others, a "vulnerability and consumer project director", two vulnerability managers, a business lead, a "performance scorecards project lead" and a team co-ordinator along with an "expert panel".

In a statement on its strategy, it says: "The UKRN facilitates co-operation and communication between its members, to promote better outcomes in economic regulation for consumers and the economy. We help our members to speak as one, where appropriate on cross cutting issues and act as a point-of-contact for engagement with consumers and stakeholders; we work together to identify and consider current and future matters of common interest, including cross-sector issues, and work together to develop consistent best practice in economic regulation; we champion the role and value of UK independent regulation through our events and publications; we make best use of expertise and resource amongst our members and we identify opportunities for working with others; we share information and experience on common issues to promote strong working relationships and collaboration; we work closely with UKCN (UK Competition Network) to support consistency across regulators with concurrent powers."

Thus, part of what this body does is to promote the role and value of independent regulation – in other words, it tells us what a useful job these regulators do.

It holds an annual conference, of course, "bringing together colleagues from across the membership of regulators". The full-day event, it says, showcases the work of the different members and the UKRN itself. And there is soon going to be a UKRN women's network.

Intriguingly, there is (at the time of writing) no information on the website (ukrn.org.uk) on how the organisation is funded or who pays for its office and staff, but in the overall scheme of regulatory matters it's probably a trifling sum. What is clear, is that "regulation" as a whole has become a successful business operation, employing thousands and spending millions – all, we are led to believe, for the common good.

And, best of all, as it's "our" money that funds the regulators, we actually pay them to tell us how good they are and what a good job they are doing. You could hardly wish for more.

From 1990 to 2010 there was a Centre for the Study of Regulated Industries (CRI), a research centre of the University of Bath School of Management. This investigated how regulation and competition were working in practice, both in the UK and abroad. It was, naturally, independent and claimed to be politically neutral.

This non-profit-making organisation was sponsored by a variety of government departments, regulators and those they regulated, including the Department for Trade and Industry and the Environment Agency, the National Audit Office, National Grid Transco, Network Rail, OfWat, Royal Mail, Thames Water, United Utilities, Wessex Water, etc.

Sadly, it is no longer with us. Some truly independent assessments would do a number of regulators a world of good.

Regulating the regulators

A (or The) Regulators' Code was issued in April 2014 under the Legislative and Regulatory Reform Act 2006. The code claims to provide "a clear, flexible and principles-based framework for how regulators should engage with those they regulate".

It was published by the "Better Regulation Delivery Office" of the Department for Business Innovation and Skills (BIS) which, in July 2016, became the Department for Business, Energy & Industrial Strategy (BEIS).

The Minister of State for Business and Enterprise at the time, Michael Fallon, wrote: "Regulators within scope of the Regulators' Code are diverse but they share a common primary purpose – to regulate for the protection of the vulnerable, the environment, social or other objective. This Code does not detract from these core purposes but seeks to promote proportionate, consistent and targeted regulatory activity through the development of transparent and effective dialogue and understanding between regulators and those they regulate."

The regulators and regulatory functions to which the Regulators' Code applies are specified in the Legislative and Regulatory Reform (Regulatory Functions) Order 2007, as amended in 2009, 2010 and 2014. Nearly all regulators, including local authorities and fire and rescue authorities, are required to pay attention to it when developing policies and procedures that guide their regulatory activities.

The Legislative and Regulatory Reform Act 2006 was extended by the Enterprise Act 2016, requiring regulators other than local authorities to formally report on the effect that the Regulators' Code has on the way they exercise their regulatory functions and the impacts of this on business; however, this had not come into force by the time of writing and there was no indication as to when it might.

While much of the code is waffle and padding, a statement was included to declare the government's commitment "to making sure it is effective".

It said: "We want businesses, regulated bodies and citizens to challenge regulators who they believe are not acting in accordance with their published policies and standards. It is in the wider public interest that regulators are transparent and proportionate in their approaches to regulation. The government will monitor published policies and standards of regulators subject to the Regulators' Code, and will challenge regulators where there is evidence that policies and standards are not in line with the Code or are not followed."

So there.

Media

The BBC: a public service in decline

What a fascinating organisation the BBC is. It started life as a company, the British Broadcasting Company Ltd, in 1922, then became a corporation following an "enquiry" which recommended it be established by Royal Charter as the British Broadcasting Corporation. The Charter, which was signed by King George V in December 1926 and which came into effect from 1st January 1927, set out the way in which the BBC would be governed.

The Charter is described as "the constitutional basis for the BBC" and is supposed to guarantee its independence. Some modifications to the Charter were made in 1931 and new, or revised, Charters introduced in 1937, 1947, 1952, 1964, 1981, 1997, 2007 and 2017. Various supplemental Charters were also introduced from time to time including, in 1969, one to transfer powers from the Postmaster General to the Minister of Posts and Telecommunications (MPT); and in 1975 changing the Ministry "responsible" from the Post Office to the MPT and then on to the Home Office.

The first Charter declared the BBC to be an instrument of education and entertainment. Subsequent Charters expanded this remit to include the dissemination of information. The eighth Charter (2007) charged the BBC with delivering the latest technology to the public and taking a leading role in the switchover to digital television, and the latest (2017) introduced major changes to the way the BBC would be run for an 11-year period.

Among the changes is that Ofcom is now "the external independent regulator" of the "independent" BBC – one of those now traditional government moves to reward a regulator for mediocrity by expanding its remit; the government can provide "guidance" to Ofcom on content requirements though editorial decisions remain the responsibility of the BBC's director-general. In addition, the National Audit Office has been given a "stronger role" in looking at how the BBC spends its money, of which it spends rather a lot.

In the year to 31st March 2017, the BBC's total income was little short of £5 billion, £3.79 billion of which came from licence fees. About £2.2 billion was spent on its television services. And it managed to write-off some £100 million on a failed project in a startling waste of licence-fee-payers' money. This was the Digital Media Initiative set up in 2008 but which never became fully operational and was scrapped in 2017; "I have serious concerns about how we managed this project," said the BBC director general at the time, Tony Hall.

So quite where is the BBC's "guaranteed independence" now? There is no doubt that some strong action was needed. The BBC had become smug and wasteful, as so often happens with organisations allowed to spend public money (given that the TV licence is effectively a tax) with few strings attached; the quality and coverage of its news broadcasts had deteriorated; it spent too much time and money on peripheral services; and rather than being a leader in broadcasting it had increasingly become a follower – and/or spoiler.

It still does a huge amount of high-quality work but...

BBC News used to be highly regarded for its independence, its wide coverage, minimal bias, careful use of words, thoroughness, objectivity, and so on. Gradually, from the mid-1970s onwards, much of this went downhill. This writer began to pay closer attention to the news reports when, in October 2011, a newsreader stated that St Paul's Cathedral in London had been "forced" to close its doors to the public.

The closure came in the midst of anti-capitalism (frequently called anti-capitalist) demonstrations by a group called "Occupy London Stock Exchange" which had set up a camp in the churchyard. It turned out that the church authorities had decided, principally on health and safety grounds, that the church should be shut. They felt they had no option – but "forced"? No one had compelled them to take this action. The BBC, however, simply read out a statement from St Paul's with no qualification whatsoever. No "St Paul's says in a statement that it has been forced to close its doors...". Other broadcasters did the same and newspapers carried the same words ... but we expect, rightly, higher standards from the BBC.

The opening ceremony of the 2012 Olympics was also illuminated by the BBC commentators' words. When athletes from Brazil entered the stadium, we were informed that Brazil was the world's largest democracy; when athletes from India marched in, we were told that India was the world's biggest democracy (or maybe Brazil was the biggest and India the largest). Silly stuff, indicating a lack of homework and the attention to detail that used to be a defining characteristic of the BBC.

Athletes from American Samoa were given worse treatment still. The presenter declared she was unable to pronounce the names of islands in this group in the South Pacific but, she continued, the capital was easier to pronounce – she then proceeded to mispronounce it spectacularly. Extraordinarily sloppy stuff. The BBC considered it did a great job of covering the Olympics – but it could have done a great deal better. Its banal interviews reached new lows, prompting one cyclist to ask his interviewer, a little rudely, "Do you know anything about cycling?"

Choice of words is important and can give a slant to a story that is undeserved. During the Iraq war, newsreaders often referred to "the holy city of Homs" without ever stating who considered it "holy". When the King of Thailand died in 2016, BBC newsreaders several times referred to him as "the much-loved king". Really! It's an offence in Thailand to be rude about the king and he was certainly popular among sectors of the population, but "much-loved"? Was that by his family, the government, the military, or the entire population?

Some of the lowest points came when a number of news broadcasts from this noble establishment led off with "news" that one of its presenters (on both radio and television programmes) was to appear in a popular dance competition. That was in 2015; in 2016 the top story on some of its bulletins was that a cookery competition would no longer be shown on the BBC but was moving to a commercial channel, while other news broadcasts discussed what the presenters of that programme would do in future. Hardly earth-shattering news – and this at a time when there were plenty of genuinely earth-shattering stories to report.

And let's not forget the corporation's treatment of one of the nation's favourite singers, Cliff Richard. Given a tip-off by South Yorkshire Police that it was about to raid a property in Berkshire owned by the entertainer, the BBC news department went overboard. A story worth about two sentences, at most, became a major story mainly because of the way the BBC handled it. This involved hiring a helicopter to try to film the raid and positioning a reporter at the entrance to the private estate. Not one useful or interesting photo or report was obtained – meaning it was a complete waste of time and money. It was a serious misjudgement – the sort of thing some of the tabloid papers are noted for. Some of them have had photographers on the spot for raids on houses of notable people following police tip-offs. But the BBC is not a tabloid organisation: it is meant to be a provider of solid, dependable, unbiased news.

The BBC was subsequently fined, compelled to pay damages to Cliff Richard and rebuked by a judge for its handling of the matter. This caused the director of BBC News and Current Affairs to claim, sniffily, that the judgment "created a significant shift in press freedom" – which it didn't – and a number of newspapers, including *The Sun*, which devoted a front page to it, made similar claims.

Back in the 1960s, one university lecturer, an émigré from Russia between the first and second world wars, told his students (this writer among them) he had observed that the better educated a nation became, the lower the standard of its reading matter. He had in mind the "condensed books" published by *Reader's Digest* but he would certainly have included papers such as *The Sun* in this. Were he still alive he would surely note the slump in standards of material shown by the BBC and others but would still be appalled by the BBC and *The Sun* being in the same camp squealing about attacks on press freedom. Over-reaction is expected from the latter; it shouldn't be the case for the former.

Those of us with televisions (or even mobile phones and computers these days) have no choice but to pay a licence fee to fund the BBC. When it comes to *The Sun* and other newspapers we have complete freedom of choice as to whether to pay to read them. I doubt I'm the only who does not wish to see their money spent in this way by the BBC, either to hire a helicopter for minimal purpose or to pay members of the legal profession to defend the indefensible in court.

Perhaps it's uncharitable to mention the hundreds of thousands of pounds worth of free publicity the BBC gives to companies such as Apple when that company launches some new gadget. Of course, no reporter would do it in exchange for a free sample ... but no doubt Apple (and others) are genuinely grateful for the plugs from such a notable non-commercial broadcaster. And the reports help fill up the "news" broadcasts.

Quite a few years back, other news broadcasters decided they should comment on news reports – in much the same way newspapers do – and eventually the BBC followed suit. Some of these comments are interesting, some well-informed, and a few give genuine insights into particular situations; but too many achieve none of these things. As Charles Moore wrote in a column in *The Spectator* in July 2017, the BBC encourages its political reporters to give "smart-arse analyses with pithy punchlines rather than just telling us what is happening".

My favourite "analysis" was a report on tensions between Israel and its neighbours: the correspondent concluded with a two-sentence summary on what had to be done to achieve peace between the Israelis and Palestinians. Brilliant. Decades, centuries even, of turmoil and hatred could be brought to an end, quickly and permanently, if only the participants would listen to these words of wisdom from a rookie reporter. Not sure if we ever heard from her again.

The BBC sometimes refers to its correspondents or reporters as "experts", which in many cases they are not. After the 2016 general election in the UK, one newsreader referred to the unexpected result which "none of our experts" had foreseen. They were, however, as accurate in their predictions as the deservedly much-maligned pollsters. However, they were in no sense "experts" – another instance of the BBC misusing words.

And here's one last example. On the morning of a meeting on neutral ground between the presidents of Russia and the United States (on 16th July 2018), a BBC commentator informed us during the breakfast programme that "the stakes could not be higher". Relations between the two countries at the time were not good and the US President had already stated he was entering talks "with low expectations". Why the BBC considered it necessary to "big up" the event is anyone's guess but the comment was the typical tosh of many commentators these days.

There are, of course, still things the BBC does particularly well. The Radio 4 programme *From Our Own Correspondent* always carries some gems. One exceptionally memorable one was from a correspondent in Venezuela who was granted access to the headquarters of a kidnap gang which brutally murdered its victims if a ransom was not paid. It was compelling stuff, an utterly brilliant and dangerous piece of investigative journalism worthy of a much wider audience than the programme commands. One hopes it received a suitable award – though it probably didn't.

State control of the airwaves

The British government has, from the beginning, kept a tighter control of airwaves than almost any other Western or developed country, with the exception of the communist nations and those ruled by dictators.

Prior to 1922, the government, through the Post Office, had steadfastly refused permission for expanding radio broadcasts in Britain, stating that they would interfere with essential services such as the armed forces – a position subsequent governments maintained until the mid-1960s. But the spectacular growth of radio broadcasts in the United States and the pressure of public opinion eventually led to the introduction of such services in the UK – all under the control of the BBC, of course.

In fact, until the early 1970s the BBC retained a legal monopoly on radio broadcasting in the UK. Despite competition in the early 1960s from Radio Luxembourg – which, horror of horrors, began beaming "pop music" into the UK – and, for a period while that was happening, the off-shore "pirate" broadcasters doing the same, it had remained the policy of both major political parties that radio was to remain under the control of the BBC.

The pirates were treated, on the flimsiest evidence, as a danger to national security and the British government did everything it could to shut them down, all while continuing to claim that there were no frequencies for other broadcasters to use. But Radio Caroline, founded in 1964 to try to break the BBC's monopoly (it was one of several offshore "pirate" broadcasters) broadcast music that large numbers of people wished to hear. The BBC simply refused to broadcast much of this music, believing its job was to treat people to classical music and educate them in its joys.

Radio Caroline, intriguingly, still exists: it used five different ships from 1964 until 1990, used satellites from 1998 to 2013 and since August 2000 has broadcast 24 hours each day via the internet and even with some restricted licences in the UK. Operating in international waters without any licence for most of its early life, it never became illegal, although the Marine Offences Act 1967 somewhat stupidly made it illegal for a British subject to associate with it.

Tony Benn (Anthony Neil Wedgwood Benn, the 2nd Viscount Stansgate who renounced the title to remain as an MP) was postmaster-general from 1964 to 1966, in Harold Wilson's Labour government, with responsibility for the BBC and broadcasting in general. He was implacably opposed to the pirate stations and also maintained the fiction that such broadcasting was a threat to national security and that there were no frequencies available for other radio stations.

After he left office, there was a change of heart by both the government and the BBC and in 1967 the BBC launched Radio 1, which quickly became its most popular radio station. Mr Benn – who apparently lived in a dream world similar to that inhabited by the character of the children's television programme of the same name – subsequently claimed that had he not banned pirate radio, Radio 1, "which brings music to far more people", would never have been created. Monopolies like to keep their monopolies intact.

After Edward Heath's government came to power in 1970, the new Minister of Post and Telecommunications, Christopher Chataway, announced a Bill to allow for the introduction of commercial radio in the United Kingdom. This service would be planned and regulated in a similar manner to the existing ITV service and would compete with the recently developed BBC Local Radio services (rather than the four national BBC services).

The new Act received Royal Assent in July 1972 and the Independent Television Authority immediately changed its name to the Independent

Broadcasting Authority and set about working towards the establishment of local radio stations in London and Glasgow, one station in each for "news and information" and one for "general and entertainment" (while still providing news bulletins). In London, LBC and Capital Radio began broadcasting in 1973 and 19 contracts had been awarded by 1976.

The BBC actually got started on regional radio broadcasts way back in 1924 with its Leeds-Bradford station but this lasted only until 1931 and it wasn't until private regional broadcasting became a possibility that the BBC took an interest in it again, launching BBC Radio Leicester in 1967, followed by a return to Leeds (without Bradford this time) in 1968. Then came stations in Stoke-on-Trent, Durham, Sheffield, Merseyside, Brighton, Nottingham and, in 1970-71, Birmingham, Bristol, Blackburn, Derby, Humberside, London, Manchester, Medway, Newcastle (replacing Durham), Oxford, Solent, and Teesside.

Initially, the stations had to be co-funded by the BBC and local authorities, which only some Labour-controlled areas proved willing to do. By the early 1970s, the local authority funding requirement was dropped and stations spread across the country, with some of the city-based stations expanding to cover a county. And now (2020) there are about 40 BBC local or regional stations covering England and the Channel Isles, with separate stations for Wales, Scotland and Northern Ireland.

With the advent of regional commercial stations, some of which have gone national, many of the BBC's local stations found themselves in competition for listeners. Some might ask why the BBC is devoting resources to such stations in the face of such competition? A good question. The answer is that the BBC, given its powerful position, is able to do this and does it simply because it can.

It took no serious interest in local radio until it looked likely that private companies could make money out of it. Similarly, the BBC showed little interest in 24-hour television until others came along; and it showed little enthusiasm for 24-hour news before other channels announced they would be doing it. It's hard to escape the conclusion that the BBC uses its power to try to prevent others gaining a foothold in the market.

The BBC began publishing *Radio Times* back in 1923 and for many years promoted it widely on both its television and radio channels. This eventually provoked complaints of unfair competition from the publishers of other listings publications. How come this non-commercial broadcaster, which was funded by a compulsory licence fee and was supposed to carry no advertising, could advertise its own magazine? This, they argued, gave it a huge advantage.

The matter went to court, as the BBC tried to defend itself against the indefensible. As a result of the case, the BBC had to sever its ties with *Radio Times*, though it was still allowed to do limited promotion.

Since 2005, following a review, no advertisements have been broadcast by the BBC for *Radio Times* or any of its other magazines. Oddly, however, it continues to promote its websites, radio stations and even apps; frequently telling us that "more news can be found on the BBC website" or on Radio BBC Whatever or "listen to the full report on BBC Radio 5". Most people, one would think, turn on the news to get the news, rather than be told where to go looking for it. Perhaps under the "regulation" of Ofcom it might cut down on such shameless promotion, but that seems unlikely.

And so to television

Britain's first television programme was launched in 1936 when there were about 100 TV sets in the country. Twenty-six years later the Television Act became law, paving the way for a commercial television service and creating the Independent Television Authority (ITA).

The ITA was expected to regulate this new service and apply certain rules, including one that commercials had to be clearly distinguishable from programmes.

This "independent" television service was named because of its independence from the independent "state" broadcaster, the BBC. And the country was to be divided into regions for each commercial broadcaster, with no national competition for the BBC. Advertising had to be sold on a region-by-region basis by each company and not on a national basis. This was because the Act required competition within the ITV system (as well as against the BBC) and sought to prevent any individual company obtaining a monopoly on commercial broadcasting.

These new broadcasters were required to provide a regional television service for their particular area, including a daily local news bulletin and regular local programming.

The first ITV contractor, Associated-Rediffusion, made its first transmission on 22nd September 1955 and others started shortly afterwards.

In preparation for the introduction of the commercial channels, the BBC broadcast its first daily television news programme in 1954: a 20-minute "illustrated summary of the news ... followed by the latest film of events and happenings at home and abroad". By the time the commercial channels got started, the BBC had doubled the amount of television time devoted to news and in September 1955 Independent Television News launched its first service.

A franchise for a nationwide breakfast television programme was awarded in 1983 to TV-am and since then the BBC and ITV have followed suit. The BBC and ITV now have competing national breakfast programmes, allocating a small proportion of the time to regional news and weather.

All the national news programmes in the UK have long since been surpassed in breadth of coverage, objectivity and on-the-spot reporting by international broadcasters such as Al Jazeera (funded by the Qatar government and based in Doha while also broadcasting from London), which also produces excellent documentaries on challenging topics. The BBC World Service used to be one of the world's most highly-respected broadcasters but it is now but a shadow of its former self, leaving a huge gap which others, such as Al Jazeera, are filling in brilliant fashion. It's remarkable how dreadful regimes can sometimes do things well.

The biggest shake-up in TV broadcasting in the UK came in 1990 with the launch of BSB which shortly afterwards became BSkyB. Satellite TV was outside the field of vision of any UK regulator and for some years did pretty much as it liked – and it is still able to beam pornographic programmes into any house which subscribes to one or other system. While viewers have to pay for lengthy spells, there are plenty of shocking 10-minute previews available to anyone.

This chapter, however, is meant to be principally about the BBC so that has to be considered elsewhere and, fortunately, the BBC hasn't felt the need to compete in this area.

Note to TV commentators on sport: we get the picture

Part of the BBC's remit is to provide unbiased coverage of events – something that is not always easy to do. But in its coverage of many sporting events, the BBC, along with most broadcasters, has simply given up on any attempt at impartiality.

The brilliant Australian cricketer and commentator, Richie Benaud, who died in 2015, drafted eight "rules of commentary": 1. never ask for a statement; 2. remember the value of a pause; 3. there are no teams in the world called "we" or "they"; 4. avoid clichés and banalities, such as "He's hit that to the boundary", "He won't want to get out now", "Of course", "As you can see on the screen"; 5. the Titanic was a tragedy, the Ethiopian drought a disaster, and neither bears any relation to a dropped catch; 6. put your brain into gear before opening your mouth; 7. concentrate fiercely at all times; 8. above all, don't take yourself too seriously, and have fun. The "rules" were meant to apply principally to cricket but could easily be adapted for other sports.

If only other commentators and supposed "expert analysts" would take note. Professional commentators have largely been sidelined by the TV channels and even some of the radio stations; instead we have former players, many with voices likely to induce boredom or sleep, doing the work and, for the most part, doing it badly.

Richie was rare: a former player who made a first-class commentator. Those of the modern era break every one of his rules with monotonous regularity, pouring forth drivel, clichés and banalities, often in a non-stop condescending tone – for instance, "the umpire/referee got that one right".

Most former cricketers, footballers and other sports "personalities" are pretty hopeless at commentary, analysis or punditry – though it can be entertaining to listen to them making prats of themselves as they drone on endlessly (or seemingly so). Unfortunately, however, the TV (and radio channels) are sold on them.

How often do we hear about players in many sports who have given a reasonably good performance being described as "absolutely magnificent"? Other favourites, among many: "He had all the time in the world", "That's unbelievable" ("unbelievable" being the most overused word of all), "How incredible is that?" Meanwhile, much of the analysis consists of telling us what has just happened while the pictures are being shown again. "That was a great move," says the commentator and the "expert analyst" will frequently respond with, "Yeah definitely (or absolutely), that was a great move." Insightful, to say the least.

Many of the television commentators tell us no more than we can see, as though unaware that we are watching the same event. Perhaps they don't understand the concept of television. Some use the future tense – e.g. he will kick for touch, this ball will go to the boundary – to describe what has already happened. Rugby sevens, rugby league and pool get the "talk far too much" awards for incessant blather but there have been several other contenders. And now snooker is getting in on the act, commentators believing that if a competitor plays a good shot, we need to be told that he (or she) has played a good shot.

Is it that the broadcasters insist on commentators and analysts (so-called) continuing to speak when they have nothing interesting or informative to say or is it simply that the speakers love the sound of their own voices? Many do no more than obey the instruction of the compère of the TV quiz show, *Catchphrase*: "Say what you see!"

In 2018 a number of letters to newspapers asked if we could possibly mute the commentary while enjoying the crowd noise, which is a great idea. Especially when the speaker says in excited tones, "And just listen to the crowd." We would love to, you moron, if only you would shut up. How great it would have been, following Liverpool's victory in the Champions League final in 2019, to hear clearly the wonderful singing of the fans; instead, we had numpties in the broadcasting box shouting banalities over the top of the singing, making what they presumably thought were important comments but adding nothing and spoiling the occasion.

Some, intriguingly, have developed a language of their own. David "Bumble" Lloyd, a cricketer turned umpire turned commentator, has been particularly adept at this. He once said of a New Zealand player, "If this bloke's a Test match bowler, then my backside is a fire engine." Couldn't say fairer than that. And it's great the way cricket commentators on TV give the score at the end of every over – in fact they give the score more often than most radio commentators – even though it is writ large (in most cases) on the bottom left of the screen. Presumably someone has told them they will sound like proper or professional commentators if they do that.

Here are a few other words and phrases that commentators regularly overuse – or really shouldn't use at all: "getting back in the game"; "playing catch-up"; "we have a game on our hands"; "under pressure", which can range from "severe" to "immense" and even "extreme"; "crucial"; "heartbreaking"; "the big man" (for any large male player); "under the pump" (don't ask!); "make no mistake"; "no doubt about it"; "I have to say"; "to be honest"; "I tell you what…"; "he can't believe it"; "he/she should have done better"; "he/she will be disappointed with that"; "long levers" (arms); "that's a great golf shot" by a golfer or "that's a great cricket shot" by a cricketer, in case we onlookers might be confused as to what sport we were watching; "this is a knowledgeable crowd" (wonderfully condescending); "that's plumb" – when it clearly isn't; "he did that well in the end" (as if the player might have taken a catch or done something else a bit sooner); "and he knows it" (after someone has made a hash of something and we might think he or she was unaware of it) – and this list could, like most commentators these days, go on and on.

It makes attending an event even more enjoyable as we can enjoy the atmosphere without having to listen to these banalities. Organisers must feel that as we are there, we don't need to be told what is going on. Such a relief.

Oh for the joy of being able to listen to a neutral, professional commentator – on radio or TV – giving us calm, informed comment on the game in progress. Please!

Ipso facto, press regulator fails to impress

IPSO is the Independent Press Standards Organisation, which describes itself as the independent regulator of most of the UK's newspapers and magazines. "We protect people's rights, uphold high standards of journalism and help to maintain freedom of expression," it states. Its vision: "A trusted, thriving, free and responsible press, reinforced by independent, effective regulation."

What does it actually do? According to its 2017 annual report, it regulates over 1,500 print and 1,500 online titles from the *Abergavenny Chronicle* to *Zoom*; takes complaints about possible breaches of the *Editors' Code of Practice*; helps with unwanted press attention or harassment concerns; provides guidance for editors and journalists and information for the public; provides advice about the *Editors' Code*; has a journalists' whistleblowing hotline and a "low cost" arbitration scheme for legal claims against the press.

A 12-member board is responsible for the oversight, vision and strategic direction of IPSO, monitoring performance and "providing advice, challenge and support". The board is also responsible for appointing the complaints committee but doesn't make decisions on complaints.

Its annual report sets out its values, declaring: it is independent – IPSO will carry out its work free from control or interference by the press, parliament, interest groups or individuals; it is bold – IPSO will act without fear or favour; it is fair – IPSO will reach judgements according to its rules based on the evidence it has gathered and its actions and sanctions will be proportionate; it is accessible – IPSO will make it as easy as possible to access its services and to engage with it; it is transparent – IPSO's work will be in the public domain, ensuring its actions and processes are clear and visible, while fulfilling any duty of confidentiality. Which are all very fine-sounding intentions.

In 2016, its second year of operation, it handled more than 14,000 complaints and enquiries. One particular complaint was made by Buckingham Palace against the *Sun* newspaper – and it was upheld, requiring the newspaper to publish the adjudication, including a front-page mention. The *Daily Mail* and the *Sun* were by far the most complained about newspapers during the year.

In 2017, the most complained about single newspaper was *The Sun* with 4,847, though the *Daily Mail* (4,176), its *Mailonline* sister (3,536) and *The Mail on Sunday* (1,452) with a combined total of 9,164 took top spot collectively. It was quite some way back to *The Metro* (1,500) and *The Times* (598); the *Daily Mirror* (120) and the *Daily Express* (110) were well behind.

IPSO is financed by the Regulatory Funding Company, which raises a levy on the news media and magazine industries. This arrangement, says the organisation, ensures secure financial support for IPSO, "while IPSO's complete independence is at the same time guaranteed by a majority of lay members, and is a further sign of the industry's commitment to effective self-regulation". In both 2015 and 2016, IPSO had a turnover of close to £2.39 million, rising a little to £2.42 million in 1917.

So that is the voluntary side of press regulation.

On the other side there is IMPRESS (Independent Monitor for the Press), which describes itself as "a regulator designed for the future of media, building on the core principles of the past, protecting journalism, while innovating to deal with the challenges of the digital age".

Its website says: "We provide journalists and publishers with the protection and the support they need to do their job, hold the powerful to account, and speak with confidence and security. We provide the public with the reassurance that they can rely on the news sources that inform them, entertain them and represent their interests."

IMPRESS also goes along with the *Editors' Code of Practice* and has an arbitration service and guidance for whistleblowers, including a hotline.

This body has been recognised by the Press Recognition Panel (PRP) as a "recognised" regulator in accordance with the Royal Charter on the Self-Regulation of the Press.

It is a "Community Interest Company" (CIC), a special type of limited company which exists to benefit the community rather than private shareholders. There is even a Regulator of Community Interest Companies, which decides whether an organisation is eligible to become, or continue to be, a community interest company. This body is responsible for investigating complaints – taking action if necessary – and it provides guidance and assistance to help people set up CICs. It works with the Department for Business, Energy & Industrial Strategy.

IMPRESS has been given the seal of the PRP as an "approved regulator". The PRP is the "independent body" set up by Royal Charter "to ensure that regulators of the UK press are independent, properly funded and able to protect the public" and it says that it works in the public interest by supporting and promoting a free press in a free and fair society. It was announced early in 2018 that it had become part of the Ministry of Justice – apparently without anyone telling it.

In its second annual report in 2017, the PRP said that IMPRESS was the only recognised regulator of the press "but a number of the larger relevant publishers remain outside the recognition system". It went on: "Several publishers have joined IPSO, which does not intend to seek recognition from the Press Recognition Panel. Other publishers have chosen not to join Impress or IPSO."

The report concludes that this situation makes it clear that there is little external incentive for publishers to join or form an approved regulator.

What a muddle! The PRP was created as a result of the Leveson Inquiry into press standards which followed "widespread concern" about unlawful activities, such as phone hacking, carried out by some sections of the media.

Lord Justice Leveson published his report into the culture, practices and ethics of the press in November 2012 and made numerous recommendations, some of which called for restrictions on press freedom and powers to be given to regulators and others to impose curbs on press activities.

In its first annual report, covering the year to 31st March 2017, IMPRESS said it regulated 69 publications, from *Arkbound* to *Your Thurrock*, had received 34 complaints and rejected all of them. In its second year it increased that number by 40 and in October 2017 it trumpeted: "High court upheld the status of IMPRESS as the first 'approved' self-regulatory body for the press in the UK."

It has a board of eight people and seven staff. Running costs in the first year were put at about £1 million, with this figure expected to rise as the workload increases; no financial details were included in its second annual report.

Some funding came from the Independent Press Regulation Trust (IPRT), set up in 2013 as a charity which exists to promote high standards of journalism. The IPRT is able to accept donations from anyone who wishes to support independent press regulation, and it can award grants to any organisation which shares this charitable purpose.

In 2015, IMPRESS entered into an agreement with the IPRT for £3.8 million in funding over a four-year period. The IPRT's funding has been guaranteed by the Alexander Mosley Charitable Trust, one of whose trustees had complained bitterly of press harassment and gave substantial evidence to the Leveson Inquiry.

IMPRESS stated that in order to safeguard its regulatory independence, it is crucial to put a firewall in place between itself and any donors. The IPRT grant can only be withdrawn in exceptional circumstances (for instance, if IMPRESS goes bankrupt) and there is no capacity for any donor to exert influence on it. "We believe that these arrangements are the best way to ensure that we are capable of fulfilling our obligations to the public, whilst protecting our independence."

So where now for press freedom – and regulation – in the UK? In April 2018, Reporters Without Borders (RSF), a Paris-based campaign group, published its 2018 World Press Freedom Index, which placed Britain in 40th place of the 180 countries considered. This was a fall of 18 places since the index had first been published in 2002 and put Britain behind all the other Western European nations apart from Italy. For the record, Norway, Sweden, The Netherlands, Finland and Switzerland were the top five; the USA was 45th, Russia was 148th and the bottom five were China, Syria, Turkmenistan, Eritrea and North Korea. The UK rose to 33rd place in 2019; North Korea, unsurprisingly, remained in last place.

Hard-won freedoms can so easily be lost. As examples of reasons for Britain's lowly place in the index, RSF referred to the new Espionage Act and the Investigatory Powers Act, plus changes in data protection legislation (aimed at limiting the scope of "public interest" defence for investigative journalism), along with strengthening the powers of a state-backed regulator.

According to Index on Censorship (a not-for-profit organisation that campaigns for and defends free expression worldwide), Britain's status as a "beacon of liberty and democracy" is being jeopardised.

In 2013, "The Royal Charter on Self-Regulation of the Press" was issued by the Privy Council. This was an odd development. The government of the day – the Coalition Government led by the Conservatives with Liberal Democrat support which was in power from 2010 to 2015 – gained sufficient cross-party support to proceed with proposals for regulating the press but decided to pursue a Charter through the Privy Council rather than introduce an Act of Parliament.

The Charter, in the customary silly language of such documents, includes the statement, ostensibly from the Queen (as that is what Royal Charters are supposed to be), "…it is in the interests of Our People that there should be a body corporate established for the purpose of determining recognition of an independent regulatory body or bodies, in pursuance of the recommendations of the Report of the [Leveson] Inquiry". The Charter said that this was in pursuit of "a new more effective policy and regulatory regime which supports the integrity and freedom of the press, the plurality of the media, and its independence, including from government, while encouraging the highest ethical and professional standards".

The "new more effective regime" was intended to replace the Press Complaints Commission, which was the "self-regulatory body" for the press for 21 years until it closed in September 2014. Its demise had been brought about by what many considered to be an inadequate response to the phone-hacking scandals that had led to the Leveson Inquiry. The government and others wanted a self-regulatory system to replace the self-regulatory system. So far, so good.

The then executive editor of *The Times* said it was "extraordinarily depressing and very, very alarming that in one short spell a hundred-year-old tradition of the press of this country, that's independent, free of political interference, has been cast aside". Other press people echoed this view; one said it would be down to newspapers to decide if they were going "to sign up to this deeply illiberal proposal or whether they should stand up for press freedom".

So the major press companies moved to set up IPSO, which the then editor of the *Spectator* said would be "the toughest regulator in the western world – which did almost everything Lord Leveson asked for but not at the behest of politicians". He added that he would be surprised if any newspapers signed up to the "new" system of regulation advocated by the government and the Royal Charter, and the then editor of *The Daily Telegraph* said (or tweeted): "Chances of us signing up for state interference: zero."

The executive director of the Society of Editors described it at the time as disappointing, saying it was a pity the Queen had been brought into controversy, before adding: "Royal charters are usually granted to those who ask for one – not forced upon an industry or group that doesn't want it."

It is certainly extremely unusual for the monarch to agree to such a controversial Charter and it is highly unlikely that Her Majesty will want to be remembered as the one who gave "her" government draconian powers to restrict press freedom. Maybe it was part of a cunning plan by the Royal family to gain revenge on parts of the press for coverage they considered too intrusive or unflattering.

Newspapers and magazines could (indeed can) choose whether to sign up to the new system of regulation, but those which do not risk exemplary damages if they lose a libel case and may also be liable to pay the complainant's costs, whether they win or lose.

Hacked Off, a lobby group which led the campaign for tighter regulation of the press, said: "News publishers now have a great opportunity to join a scheme that will not only give the public better protection from press abuses but will also uphold freedom of expression, protect investigative journalism and benefit papers financially. The press should seize the chance to show the public they do not fear being held to decent ethical standards, and that they are proud to be accountable to the people they write for and about." As in so many fields, everyone seemed to be saying much the same thing about what should be done but with substantial disagreements as to how it should be achieved.

The position in June 2018 was that the majority of publishers and publications were members of IPSO, which might be described as the unofficial regulator but is proving to be highly effective; while a small proportion belonged to the officially sanctioned regulator, which is dependent on donations, and which, though it might eventually prove to be effective, will almost certainly never achieve the status intended by the Royal Charter or sought by numerous politicians and lobby groups. It is rare for Royal Charters to be so unappreciated or so greatly ignored by the people they are intended for – but then everything about this one was unusual.

"Self-regulation" obviously means different things to different people. It appears to be a bit like the Chinese Government's (hollow) commitment to the status of Hong Kong after it gained independence in 1997: "One nation, two systems."

There were other "solutions" available: the Press Complaints Commission could easily have been reformed, or Ofcom, which exists to regulate "communications", could have had "press" added to its already very wide remit, although given its performance elsewhere that would almost certainly have been a backwards step.

Controlling standards in advertising

Back in 1955, when commercial TV started, the advertising was controlled by legislation – the first time that advertisements had been subject to any formal regulation. When commercial radio began in 1973, the ads broadcast were also subject to statutory control.

In 1961, the Committee of Advertising Practice (CAP) was set up by the advertising "industry"; this produced the first edition of the *British Code of Advertising Practice*. In 1962, CAP established the Advertising Standards

Authority (ASA) – which still exists – as the independent advertising regulator under the code.

In 1974, the industry set up the Advertising Standards Board of Finance (Asbof) "to provide sufficient and secure funding" through a levy of 0.1% on advertising space costs for the ASA not only to function but also to promote itself to the public.

In 1988, the Control of Misleading Advertisements Regulations provided the ASA with legal backing from the Office of Fair Trading (OFT) – a non-ministerial department which existed from 1973 to 2014 when its responsibilities were passed to a number of different organisations. These regulations enabled the ASA to refer advertisers who made persistent misleading claims and refused to co-operate with the self-regulatory system to the OFT for legal action.

The ASA can still refer "problem advertisers" for unfair or misleading advertising, but now under the Consumer Protection from Unfair Trading Regulations 2008 and the Business Protection from Misleading Marketing Regulations 2008, which replaced the Control of Misleading Advertisements Regulations 1988. Then in 2013, responsibility for legal back-up transferred from the Office of Fair Trading to Trading Standards, a body (with national and regional offices) set up by the government in 2012 as part of changes to "the consumer protection landscape".

The ASA states: "Referral to Trading Standards is a last resort and rarely needed: the overwhelming majority of advertisers work within the system."

In 2004, the ASA/CAP system took over the responsibility for TV and radio ads. The newly-formed communications regulator, Ofcom, decided (in a move supported by parliament) to contract-out responsibility for broadcast (TV and radio) advertising to the ASA system in a co-regulatory partnership, creating a single regulator for advertising.

A new industry committee, the Broadcast Committee of Advertising Practice, was created to write and maintain the Broadcast Advertising Code. The Broadcast Advertising Standards Board of Finance (Basbof) was established to collect the 0.1% levy on broadcast advertising space costs and an ASA (Broadcast) was launched to administer the codes.

From under 100 complaints in its first year of operation, the ASA now receives over 30,000 a year. This, says the ASA, is mainly due to the fact that the ASA is well known, that it has a much broader remit and that it is easier to complain. It adds that the system is continuing to develop, based on the principles that ads should not mislead, harm or offend.

In 1995, the ASA's remit was expanded to cover advertisements in "non-broadcast electronic media", predominantly in paid-for online promotions such as banner and display ads and paid-for searches.

By 2007 the internet had become the second most-complained about medium and the ASA was turning away nearly two-thirds of the complaints it received about online advertising because they related to claims made on companies' own websites, which were not subject to the rules. In 2010, CAP announced the extension of the ASA's online remit to cover these.

Today, the authority says, advertising in the UK overwhelmingly sticks to the rules. Its compliance surveys regularly reveal that more than 97% of ads are in line with the Advertising Codes.

That's a lengthy introduction to the state of things today in the regulation of advertisements. Is this "regulation" working? Not as far as ads by certain other regulators are concerned. The misleading ads for workplace pensions (*referred to in a later section*) did not spur any action from the ASA and nor do "false" ads on Facebook or other social media sites.

The founder of the MoneySavingExpert.com website, Martin Lewis, felt compelled in April 2018 to take legal action against Facebook for allowing ads to appear which carried his name and photo but which were scams that took many people in, causing losses of up to £100,000. Mr Lewis declared, repeatedly, that he had not placed any ads on Facebook.

A Facebook spokesman was quoted in *The Times* as saying: "We do not allow adverts on Facebook which are misleading or false." But that is simply not true. Otherwise the ads would not appear. And Facebook, which gets paid by the scammers, puts the responsibility on people such as Mr Lewis to report the ads before it considers removing them. It's entirely wrong – and where is the ASA in all this? Nowhere. But then, if you want the ASA to take action, you have to lodge a complaint and the ASA doesn't have the resources or the ability to tackle scammers. Facebook does – but doesn't do it effectively.

In 2016, the ASA "resolved" 28,521 complaints resulting in 4,824 ads (a record at the time) being changed or withdrawn. In the same year CAP delivered 281,061 pieces of advice and training to the industry to help them get their ads "right". Income was £8.6 million, £5.6 million of which was spent on salaries and direct staff costs.

In 2018, it "secured" the withdrawal or amendment of 10,850 ads or ad campaigns; CAP delivered more than half a million pieces of advice and training; "resolved" complaints had risen to 33,727, 98% of them from the public. Income was up to £9.34 million and operating expenditure £9.28 million.

The ASA together with the CAP claim they have "adapted to make ads responsible wherever they appear", but whatever progress they have made, there is still a very long way to go. It acknowledges, however, that "responsible advertisements are good for people, society and businesses" – and you couldn't say fairer than that.

Money

Can we bank on regulation?

For some years it was hard to know if the Governor of the Bank of England was modelled on the fictional character of the television comedy *Yes Prime Minister* or if it was the other way around. Sir Desmond Glazebrook (the fictional one who wanted the job) had a phenomenal repertoire of clichés; the real Governor was not far behind, especially when all sorts of crises arose during the period from 2006 to 2010.

The financial regulatory system in the UK at that time was a tripartite structure with responsibility shared between the Bank of England, the Treasury and the Financial Services Authority.

The Bank of England, being the UK's central bank, has two main functions: (1) to ensure monetary stability to keep prices as stable as possible, thus maintaining confidence in the currency; and (2) to maintain financial stability by identifying and where possible reducing threats posed against the financial system as a whole.

The so-called banking crisis of that era, accompanied by several other factors highly damaging to the economy, was quite a long time coming and it's hard to escape the impression that the Bank of England had been asleep on the job.

It should have been aware, for instance, that banks were engaging in highly dubious practices. Not least of these was the way they were buying packs of high-risk mortgages from lenders in the USA – American mortgage lenders and brokers had adopted the bookmakers' art of laying off risky investments (or wagers) – and also assisting, with a subsidiary of the soon-to-be-defunct Lehman Brothers, in dealings with these "sub-prime" as well as "near-prime" mortgages.

When the US housing market suffered a catastrophic drop – something which had been largely unanticipated, as pundits ignored the old adage that what goes up generally comes down again – these sub-prime mortgages lost the bulk of their worth and Northern Rock, which had started life as a Newcastle upon Tyne-based building society, was caught out in particular. It sought help from the government but, when news of this leaked out, people queued to withdraw their money and the bank collapsed, thus becoming the first British bank in 150 years to fail because of a bank run. In February 2008 the government nationalised it to stave off insolvency.

It wasn't the only bank to fall foul of the collapse in the US housing market but, because of its size, it was the most vulnerable. It may have been that this bank (and others) didn't appreciate the difference in the way mortgage defaults were handled between the two countries. In the UK, mortgage lenders seek to reclaim every penny of the money they have lent from those they have granted mortgages to; but in America people can simply walk away from properties and the mortgages they can no longer afford to pay. No one pursues them for the balance should the sale of a repossessed or abandoned property not pay off the loan.

The Bank of England should have been awake to these dodgy dealings – and possibly worse scams and unscrupulous actions by several other banks – and taken some action or at least issued warnings. The Bank was also reportedly advised of shenanigans with LIBOR, the average interbank interest rate at which a number of banks on the London money market are prepared to lend to one another from terms as short as overnight to as much as 12 months. The rate is announced once each working day and is used as a base rate by banks and other financial institutions. Rises and falls can affect interest rates on various banking products such as savings accounts, mortgages and loans.

Years later people were fined for their part in attempting (and sometimes apparently succeeding) to manipulate the rate for their own gain. Had the Bank acted when it was made aware of the "problem", it might have preserved at least some of the integrity of the financial markets.

The Bank might, perhaps reasonably, claim that it had no responsibility with regards to "payment protection insurance" (PPI). Banks began selling PPI policies, often somewhat aggressively, alongside mortgages, loans and credit cards during the 1990s. They were meant to enable borrowers to repay what they owed if their income fell because they became ill or lost their jobs.

The policies proved highly profitable for the banks, as barely 15% of the income was paid out – making PPI much more lucrative than car or house insurance. The major high street banks made huge profits from it, as the premiums often added 20% to the cost of a loan and in some cases more than 50%.

The Financial Services Authority (which no longer exists) began imposing fines for mis-selling the insurance in 2006 and three years later it banned one of the worst types of PPI: single premium policies that were being sold to mortgage-buyers and added to their total loan at the start.

Things really took off in 2008 after *Which?* reported that one in three PPI customers had been sold "worthless" insurance – a turn for the better, one might say. Eventually, banks were compelled to examine thousands of claims for PPI mis-selling and work through their past PPI sales to find customers who deserved compensation. Lloyds had about a third of the PPI market, followed by Royal Bank of Scotland (RBS) with 18%.

The FSA had estimated that around 3 million people could be eligible for PPI refunds, worth a total of £4.5 billion, but the final bill is likely to exceed £20 billion, really hitting the banks where it hurts at a time when they have been struggling to get their balance sheets in order after all the crises of the "noughties" – or "naughties" as far as many of them were concerned.

The Financial Conduct Authority, a replacement body for the FSA, eventually set August 2019 as the final date for claims of mis-selling to be lodged. This brought a degree of certainty to the banking industry and the share prices of Lloyds, RBS, Barclays and others rose on the announcement.

Following the crisis of 2008 onwards, the government announced a number of proposed changes to the financial regulatory structure with the Bank of England becoming the single authority with responsibility for preserving financial stability and providing protection to the wider economy as a whole – an odd reward for failure. In addition, the FSA was replaced by three new bodies: the Financial Policy Committee (FPC), the Prudential Regulation Authority (PRA) and the Financial Conduct Authority (FCA).

The FPC is a committee of the governing body of the Bank of England with responsibility for macro-prudential regulation, concentrating on the stability of the financial sector as a whole. It has three main functions: (1) to monitor the economic system to identify risks to the financial stability of the economy; (2) to take action to address any such risks; (3) to communicate to parliament and the public its analysis of the situation and the actions it has taken.

The Bank of England also has a Monetary Policy Committee. According to the Bank, monetary policy is "the process by which the Bank of England sets the interest rate – and sometimes carries out other measures – in order to reach a target rate of inflation".

The Bank has (or certainly had) a childishly simplistic definition of "inflation" on its website, which reads: "Inflation is the rate of increase in the prices of goods and services. It is expressed as a percentage. If inflation is 3%, this means that, on average, the price of goods and services is 3% higher than it was a year earlier.

"Limited inflation encourages people to spend sooner, which is good for economic growth – if consumers or business anticipate that prices will fall in the future, they are likely to hold off on spending.

"Every month, a team of specialists from the Office for National Statistics (ONS) collects around 180,000 separate prices of about 700 items covering everything from food and drink to clothes, furniture and train fares. This 'basket of goods' is used to calculate the Consumer Prices Index (CPI). The ONS publishes an updated rate every month. This is the inflation measure used in the government's inflation target (but there are other measures of inflation).

"Generally, when people feel like spending – in other words when demand for goods and services exceeds supply – inflation tends to rise. When people don't feel like spending and supply exceeds demand, inflation tends to fall.

"So to meet the inflation target, our Monetary Policy Committee (MPC) changes the official Bank of England interest rate (also known as Bank Rate or the Base Rate). This is the rate of interest that we pay on reserves held by commercial banks at the Bank of England. Generally, banks pass these changes on to customers. So if we raise Bank Rate, these customers tend to receive more interest on savings and/or pay more interest on debt like loans and credit cards, and vice versa.

"So, if inflation looks set to go above target we would probably increase interest rates so people spend less, which tends to reduce inflation. Or if inflation looks likely to fall below target we would probably cut interest rates to boost spending in the economy and help inflation to rise.

"If we miss the inflation target by more than 1 percentage point either side – in other words, if the CPI inflation rate is more than 3% or less than 1% – the Governor of the Bank of England must write a letter to the Chancellor. This letter explains why inflation has increased or fallen and what the Bank of England proposes to make sure it comes back to target."

Fascinating stuff. It's a totally different definition of "inflation" from what used to be taught in economics courses at universities, where inflation was related to increases in the supply of money in the economy.

The CPI is a curious assessment, which takes no account of housing costs, a major factor in the lives of vast numbers of people. Nevertheless, it's the index that is most commonly used and it affects all sorts of things.

For many years the Retail Prices Index (RPI) was used. This was first calculated in the early 20th century and went under various names such as the Index of Retail Prices and the General Index of Retail Prices. Then came the RPIX, leaving mortgage interest rates out of the RPI.

An explicit target for inflation was introduced in 1992 by the Chancellor of the Exchequer, Norman Lamont, and this was based on the RPIX. Interest rates at that time were set by the Treasury but shortly after the Labour party came to power in 1997, the new Chancellor, Gordon Brown, passed this responsibility to the Bank of England, specifically the Monetary Policy Committee. This committee was given (and still has) the responsibility of adjusting interest rates in order to meet an inflation target *set by the Chancellor*. The initial target rate of inflation was set at an RPIX of 2.5%.

In January 2013 the Office for National Statistics decided that the RPI did not meet international standards but it still collects and publishes figures for this, with the disclaimer that it is "not a national statistic", although, weirdly, this measure of "inflation" is still used in various calculations by government departments.

In 1996, the Conservative government introduced the Consumer Price Index, which was intended to replace the RPI, and in 2003 the government's inflation target was changed from the RPIX of 2.5% to the CPI of 2%.

Unlike the RPI, the CPI takes the "geometric" mean of prices to aggregate items at the lowest levels, instead of the "arithmetic" mean, which usually means that the CPI will be lower than the RPI. This is because of the perfectly reasonable assumption that people will buy less of something if its price goes up and more if its price goes down – a very basic law of economics, even if consumers don't always actually act in this way.

CPI has been criticised as being a less effective measure of price rises than the RPI, on the basis that it is easier to manipulate and less broadly based, but in 2010 the new Tory Chancellor, George Osborne, declared that CPI was to be more widely adopted, including for setting benefits and pensions.

But back to the setting of interest rates. This is the main (in fact just about the only) instrument the Monetary Policy Committee has to try to regulate inflation. Following the various problems of 2008-09, the MPC, along with equivalent bodies in the USA and later in the EU, painted itself, somewhat comically, into a corner by reducing interest rates to near zero. Not only was it fun to watch but it was brilliant for people with mortgages, particularly large ones, who found themselves paying much less than they had anticipated and went on doing so for the next decade – and who knows for how long it might still continue? The MPC and, more particularly, the hapless Governor of the Bank of England, kept warning that interest rates would have to rise but just couldn't bring themselves to take the plunge.

Coupled with its moronic policy on interest rates, the MPC introduced what it called "quantitative easing", which is effectively printing money to help financial institutions to get their houses back in order. The Americans, followed by the European Central Bank, adopted a similar method of trying to restore order. In times past, many governments have "printed" money to stimulate economies and spend their way out of recessions – this money was usually spent on infrastructure projects to the benefit of large sectors of society. But not this time.

The Bank of England describes it as "an unconventional form of monetary policy" designed "to stimulate the economy when interest rates are already low" with the ultimate aim of "boosting spending to reach our inflation target of 2%". It adds: "Quantitative easing does not involve literally printing more money. Instead, we create new money digitally."

By mid-2018, not far short of £450 billion had been "created" this way in the UK. A pretty substantial sum and had it been invested in infrastructure projects it would certainly have brought much-needed benefits to the country as a whole, rather than just to financial institutions. Even a small proportion of it would have helped greatly.

Such artificial increases in the money supply are always inflationary, so inflation remained above the government's target for long spells but both the Treasury and the Bank were happy with this, even though vast swathes of the population were not – especially those in public services such as the NHS who had their wages held back year after year by government policy and became substantially worse off financially in real terms.

The policies pursued by the Treasury and the Bank were little short of the standards set by what are commonly known as "banana republics" and most of us could do no more than watch as the rich got richer (often substantially) and the low-paid got poorer and poorer.

Another triumph of regulation!

Looking after financial services – and "our" money

The Financial Conduct Authority (FCA) describes itself as an independent financial regulator which is accountable to the Treasury and parliament. The Treasury appoints a board with 11 members which "manages and challenges our senior executives, helps hold us to account and helps set our direction as an organisation".

It says: "We are the conduct regulator for the whole of the UK financial services industry and the prudential regulator for 18,000 authorised firms."

The FCA does not receive funding from the government as it funds the cost of delivering its statutory objectives by raising fees from the firms it regulates – with some of it coming from penalties imposed on firms which have been naughty, although the bulk of that money goes to the Treasury. Penalties of £189.2 million were collected in 2016-17 (down from £877.2 million the previous year), of which £148.7 million (£843.1 million the previous year) was paid to the Exchequer. Its total income in 2016-17 was £566.3 million (£543.9 million from fees) and it spent £321.9 million of that on its staff who operate in offices in London and Edinburgh.

According to the chairman's report in the 2016-17 annual report, the FCA works on the basis that the best form of regulation is preventative (presumably meaning "preventive", but it's optional) – what he calls "constructive deterrence". One of its duties is to carry out an investigation and report to the Treasury if there has been a significant regulatory failure.

The stated aims of the FCA are "to protect consumers, ensure the industry remains stable and promote healthy competition between financial services providers".

It maintains the Financial Services Register, which is a public record of firms, individuals and other bodies that are, or have been, regulated by the FCA and/or the PRA – the PRA being the Prudential Regulation Authority through which the Bank of England "prudentially regulates and supervises" about 1,500 financial services firms. "Prudential regulation" is a type of financial regulation that requires financial firms to control risks and hold adequate capital as defined by "capital requirements".

Banks, building societies, investment firms, credit unions and insurers are required to provide regulatory returns to the PRA. "We work with the FCA to make sure the regulatory reporting processes for dual-regulated firms are efficient," the PRA states. The authority is structured as a limited company wholly owned by the Bank of England.

The PRA and the FCA are the successors to the Financial Services Authority, a quasi-judicial body responsible for the regulation of the financial services industry in the UK between 2001 and 2013, which began life as the Securities and Investments Board in 1985.

Then there is OPBAS (The Office for Professional Body Anti-Money Laundering Supervision), a new regulator set up in December 2017 by the government to strengthen the UK's anti-money laundering (AML) supervisory regime and to "ensure the professional body AML supervisors provide consistently high standards of AML supervision". According to the Treasury, it has been created to further tighten the UK's defences against money laundering and terrorist financing.

It says that it was set up as part of a wider package of reforms to strengthen the AML supervisory regime in the UK. The OPBAS Regulations 2018 came into effect in January 2018, giving OPBAS duties and powers to ensure the AML supervisors meet the standards required by the Money Laundering Regulations 2017. OPBAS is housed within the FCA and facilitates collaboration and information sharing between the professional body AML supervisors, statutory supervisors and law enforcement agencies.

It aims to improve the consistency of professional body AML supervision in the accountancy and legal sectors but does not directly supervise legal and accountancy firms.

The professional body AML supervisors overseen by OPBAS were/are (in May 2018): Association of Accounting Technicians, Association of Chartered Certified Accountants, Association of International Accountants, Association of Taxation Technicians, Chartered Institute of Legal Executives, Chartered Institute of Management Accountants, Chartered Institute of Taxation, Council for Licensed Conveyancers, Faculty of Advocates, Faculty Office of the Archbishop of Canterbury, General Council of the Bar/Bar Standards Board, General Council of the Bar of Northern Ireland, Insolvency Practitioners Association, Institute of Certified Bookkeepers, Institute of Chartered Accountants in England and Wales, Institute of Chartered Accountants in Ireland, Institute of Chartered Accountants of Scotland, Institute of Financial Accountants, International Association of Bookkeepers, Law Society/Solicitors Regulation Authority, Law Society of Northern Ireland and Law Society of Scotland.

OPBAS does not supervise members of professional bodies, such as firms of accountants and solicitors, or any other type of business subject to the requirements of the Money Laundering Regulations 2017; statutory anti-money laundering supervisors such as the Gambling Commission and HM Revenue and Customs; activity carried out by professional body supervisors outside the UK; and the adequacy of any functions performed by professional body supervisors unrelated to AML supervision – this includes any oversight of their members' controls over other types of financial crime, such as those related to the prevention of fraud, improving data security and the implementation of financial sanctions and asset freezes.

It is only to be hoped that OPBAS can keep track of what it is supposed to be doing or not doing, which in itself would be quite an achievement. To date, the bulk of money laundering counteraction has affected "the little people", those who didn't have much to begin with but who have to provide evidence of where their trifling sums have come from. Meanwhile, most money laundering, involving huge transfers of ill-gotten gains, continues virtually unabated. It is yet another of those areas where a great deal of activity by regulators inconveniences the innocent while scarcely troubling the guilty.

Here is a suggestion for regulating much of the activity of banks, especially the so-called merchant ones. As the bulk of their money-making ventures amount to gambling – whether on currency, stock exchange or commodity movements – why not shift the responsibility for regulating this to the Gambling Commission?

This body might be better suited to restricting the activities of "rogue traders" such as Nick Leeson, a derivatives and futures trader whose fraudulent, unauthorised, speculative and unchecked risk-taking caused the collapse of Barings Bank in 1995. It would give the Gambling Commission more of an international role. And it might help to make it clear that most of the so-called wealth creators in the UK turn out to be nothing more than gamblers on a large scale. Gamblers whose losses often end up being underwritten by the government.

Keeping a careful eye on what is spent

The National Audit Office (NAO) is an independent parliamentary body which is responsible for auditing central government departments, government agencies and non-departmental public bodies. It also carries out value for money (VFM) audits with regard to the administration of public policy. Its motto is: "Helping the nation spend wisely."

Formed in 1983, it has nearly 800 employees – who are not classed as civil servants – and an annual budget approaching £65 million. Its work led, it says, to audited savings of £1.21 billion in 2015; but in its 2017-18 annual report it recorded audited savings of a mere £741 million. It stated: "We certified the accounts of all government departments, including big commercial entities such as the BBC, Network Rail and financial service companies, and many other public-sector bodies, covering more than £1.6 trillion of public income and expenditure."

The head of the NAO is known as the Comptroller and Auditor General and is also an independent officer of the House of Commons.

The NAO is overseen by the Public Accounts Commission (PAC), a parliamentary committee of MPs, which: approves its budget; scrutinises costs and performance; appoints external auditors; and commissions value-for-money studies of the NAO's work.

It would be useful to have a body which vetted spending on large projects, especially those related to IT, *before* money was spent. During the 1990s, an average of about £500 million was wasted each year on hardware and software that either didn't work or, more commonly, was not up to the job. Some government departments and agencies actually abandoned systems before they were switched on. This waste of money steadily increased during the first two decades of the 21st century with massive overspends on numerous projects, several of which finally proved to be not suitable for the work for which they were intended. HMRC's overspend – its system cost well over £8 billion after budgeting for about £2.6 billion – eclipsed all but the national one for the NHS – but the HMRC one did eventually work after a raft of "teething problems".

The one project where a proper inquiry took place was unrelated to computers: it was instead concerned with the Scottish Parliament building. Initial estimates ranged from an unrealistic £10 million to a more plausible £40 million, but the final cost turned out to be £414 million. The public inquiry found there had been failings throughout the project; construction started in June 1999 and should have been completed in 2001; however, it took a further three years.

One finding of the inquiry was that those responsible for running the project had acted outside their areas of competence – or words to that effect. And that has been the problem with virtually every computer system installed in government departments, agencies, quangos, even regulators: those responsible for procurement, mainly civil servants, have acted outside their areas or spheres of competence.

Local authorities were hit as well. The Community Charge ("Poll Tax"), Mrs Thatcher's baby, was introduced in Scotland in 1989 and England and Wales in 1990 (it was not implemented in Northern Ireland). It broke almost every "rule" of taxation, being hugely regressive and highly expensive to collect, to name but two. These factors were well known but Mrs Thatcher was not one to be easily deterred, whether because of stubbornness or stupidity. Local councils had to be able to send letters to everyone over the age of 18 in their communities and in areas with substantial numbers of students present for little more than half a year and living elsewhere for the rest, it was a complicated task to get them to pay.

Many councils had to install new computer systems to enable them to deal with the vast increase in correspondence, systems that were not needed for much other work. It was great for the suppliers of hardware and software but no one else. The tax might even have worked for a while had not considerable numbers of people refused to pay, forcing councils to spend considerable sums pursuing them through the courts.

The abolition of the tax was announced in March 1991, by which time John (now Sir John) Major was the Prime Minister. About this time, the Chancellor of the Exchequer, Norman Lamont (now Baron Lamont of Lerwick), increased the rate of VAT from 15% to 17.5% to try to make up for the shortfall on local authority finances brought about by the tax.

A brilliant article published in the *Sunday Times* shortly afterward was called "Mark well the cost of the poll tax"; the author, Robert Harris (if memory serves well), reckoned that the tax had sucked some £10 billion out of local authority finances. The tax was an incredibly expensive folly with, despite some protestations from people who were cabinet members at the time, absolutely nothing in its favour.

The NAO may well have conducted an audit on this folly – or it may not. Such a shame if it didn't. Had the amounts wasted by this tax, computer installations, and buildings (such as the Scottish Parliament and others) been better spent, we might well have avoided the period of austerity ushered in by the Chancellor, George Osborne, in 2010.

In June 2018 the NAO gave a scathing, withering assessment of the government's "universal credit" system, stating it "has not – and may never – deliver value for money". It was intended to reduce, in fact substantially reduce, welfare payments, but the NAO said the single payment scheme might cost more than the benefits system it replaced; and added that it might never be known if it has achieved its stated goal of increasing employment.

The "universal credit" was intended to consolidate benefits such as tax credits, unemployment and housing benefit into one monthly payment, to simplify the benefits system and to provide added incentive for claimants to find employment.

The NAO report echoed long-held criticisms voiced by opponents but the government simply ignored all adverse comments and pressed on with its dog's breakfast of a scheme and awarded a knighthood at the beginning of 2020 to one of its principal architects, one Iain Duncan Smith.

Keeping track of what MPs spend

The Independent Parliamentary Standards Authority (IPSA) was established in May 2010 to regulate MPs' business costs and expenses, determine MPs' pay and pension arrangements, and provide financial support to MPs in carrying out their parliamentary functions. Its work is funded by the Treasury.

It is governed by a board, which consists of a chairperson and four members: one of whom must be a person who has held high judicial office; one a qualified auditor; and one a former MP.

IPSA is, however, run by its chief executive and directors, who report to the Board, supported by an executive body of staff – more than 60 of them – who are responsible for administering, regulating and paying MPs' business costs and expenses. With 650 members of parliament, that's just about one IPSA staff member per 10 MPs – which might to the untrained eye (or even a trained one) seem somewhat excessive.

The aim, says IPSA, is to assure the public that MPs' use of taxpayers' money is well regulated and that MPs are resourced appropriately to carry out their parliamentary functions.

In the financial year 2018-19, IPSA spent just short of £4 million on its own staff, while dealing with MPs' pay, staffing, business costs and expenses totalling a little over £190 million. Good value all round, surely.

Taking some sort of care of some pensions

The Pensions Regulator (TPR) is the UK regulator of workplace pension schemes.

"We make sure that employers put their staff into a pension scheme and pay money into it," it says. "We also make sure that workplace pension schemes are run properly so that people can save safely for their later years." Its vision, it states in its annual report for 2018-19, is "of being a strong, agile, fair and efficient regulator".

It is led by a board which meets eight times a year and is made up of a "non-executive chair", six non-executive directors, a chief executive and two executive directors. All the members are appointed by the Secretary of State for Work and Pensions, "following open competition".

Spending in 2016-17 was £74.8 million, up from £62.8 million the year before; by 2018-19 it had risen to £85.4 million and it expects this to reach £110.2 million in 2020-21. The average number of full-time equivalent people employed during 2016-17 was 527 (up from 503 in 2015-16), costing nearly £37.5 million; this rose to 675 people at a cost of £50.17 million in 2018-19.

This regulatory body was established by the Pensions Act 2004 "to support the strategic aims of the Department for Work and Pensions". Its main purpose is to regulate work-based pension schemes and to "support employers in complying with their automatic enrolment duties in relation to those schemes".

"Workplace pensions" was a neat trick by the government. Pensions used to be (in fact still are) paid out from a portion of the National Insurance contributions paid in by employees (for most, 12% in 2018-19 on wages of £162.01 to £892 a week) and employers (13.8% on those wages). That's a hefty tax. But with all the other demands on government spending, it's not enough to pay pensions indefinitely.

Rather than raise the levels of taxation, the government transferred much of the responsibility to the private sector. Employers have to set up pension schemes for their staff. There is an option for employees to opt out but the aim is to have most employed people enrolled in a "workplace" pension scheme to prepare for their retirement.

In essence, says the government website, if you're in a defined contribution pension scheme, each payday you put in £40, your employer puts in £30, you get £10 tax relief, so a total of £80 goes into your pension. By doing this, the government neatly avoided raising taxes to fund pensions – by "taxing" employers and employees for the considerable benefit of private companies. Brilliant. And by keeping NI contributions at their existing levels.

Minimum contributions were set at 3% of wages per employee topped up with 2% from the employer but from April 2019 these rose to 5% and 3% respectively. The money, instead of going into the relative safety of the government coffers, goes into private sector companies which have to be approved by the pensions regulator. All this money going into the private sector will inevitably mean there will be scams, losses, money misappropriated and all the other failings that pensions schemes have shown in the past. Look no further than Equitable Life and the problems it caused for the many thousands of people who had looked forward to a reasonable lifestyle in their retirement years.

There is now a "safety net" to protect people in the workplace schemes but we are yet to see how this will work. This writer had cause to write to the Pensions Regulator over a small matter and the response came with his name misspelt. There was no apology forthcoming when the error was pointed out, just a terse statement that a correction had been made. But if the regulator can't get minor details correct – and think what problems a misspelt name could cause years down the line – what hope is there of it getting the big stuff right?

The regulator mounted several advertising campaigns to get employers and employees interested. An early one featured considerable numbers of workers declaring, "We're all benefitting from workplace pensions." This was at a time when no one had benefitted, unless taking home less money each week (or month) could be considered a benefit.

Intriguingly, these ads appeared at a time when the Advertising Standards Authority (ASA) was running its own advertising campaign pointing out the need for advertisements to be "legal, decent, honest and truthful". While the Pensions Regulator's ads may have been legal and decent, they most certainly were not honest or truthful, but the ASA took no action against them. One regulator taking on another? It couldn't happen!

A later wave of advertising featured a grotesque, lumbering monster urging people who might not have considered such pensions to get involved. Whether intentionally or not (probably not), the monster came across as a metaphor for the entire scheme.

In May 2016, the chief economist at the Bank of England told an audience of bankers and politicians that, despite considering himself moderately financially literate, he was unable to make the remotest sense of pensions. He added: "Conversations with countless experts and independent financial advisers have confirmed for me only one thing: that they have no clue either."

One can only hope the Pensions Regulator has a better handle on things – but that is probably unlikely.

Justice

Court out: you might be lucky ... or not

Back in 1988, the Master of the Rolls, Lord Denning, stated: "It is better that some innocent men remain in jail than that the integrity of the English judicial system be impugned."

That's one of the most chilling statements made by a senior judge in the last 50 years. In other words, "We don't care if the judicial system sends innocent people to jail so long as we can keep doing what we've been doing."

It is somewhat reminiscent of North Vietnam's Ho Chi Minh whose National Liberation Front believed it was "better that a possible innocent man dies than that a guilty man escapes".

Note that Lord Denning was referring to the English system – not British. Scotland, in particular, has a system that is superior in many respects but try telling that to the Ministry of Justice in London. The Scottish system makes rather more concerted efforts to establish "facts" and "truth". And it has a high degree of integrity, something the English judicial system has not had much of for many hundreds of years. Perhaps Lord Denning was urging us to hang on to the last remaining shreds of it.

The quaintly titled Master (or Keeper) of the Rolls and Records of the Chancery of England is the second most senior judge in England and Wales after the Lord Chief Justice and serves as President of the Civil Division of the Court of Appeal and Head of Civil Justice. Lord Denning (1899-1999), born Alfred Thompson Denning and known as Tom, made numerous controversial statements during his legal career, including a number during his time in the near top job. He was made a member of the Order of Merit in 1997.

For instance, he suggested that some immigrants might not be suitable as jurors; he felt that if the "Birmingham Six" had been hanged, "they'd have been forgotten and the whole community would have been satisfied" – he said this even though they were subsequently released; in a civil action brought by those six against the police for injuries they received in police custody he said that "to accept that the police were lying would open an appalling vista" but 11 years later he admitted he was wrong, saying the West Midlands detectives had "let us all down".

After his death, the Lord Chief Justice, Lord Bingham, said: "Lord Denning was the best known and best loved judge of this, or perhaps any, generation. He was a legend in his own lifetime."

A legend indeed and one who must bear considerable responsibility for the appalling state of the English judicial system. In so many ways it stinks. At the highest level, it's appallingly, disgracefully smug. And it's a national disgrace that so many innocent people have been sent to jail in the last 40 years...

Take the case of Hilda Murrell, a 78-year-old anti-nuclear campaigner who was abducted and murdered in 1984. The young man – he was 16 when the crimes took place – convicted of the crimes was not only very unlikely to have committed them on his own but was almost certainly incapable of so doing. He was convicted on police evidence and was still in prison in 2019. It was largely a case of being in the wrong place at the wrong time and a convenient person to charge to bring a bizarre case to a close. But there have been a vast number of miscarriages of justice in the last 50 years and one wonders how they could continue to occur under a legal system that was once considered, and is still proclaimed by some, to be the best in the world.

It was the case for many years that appeals against convictions would only be considered if the defence could come up with "new evidence". Usually there couldn't be any "new" evidence. What was actually required was a proper appraisal of the evidence that had either been presented at the trial or withheld by the prosecution. Eventually, because so many miscarriages of justice were being highlighted by campaigners, the government set up the Criminal Cases Review Commission (CCRC) in 1995: an "independent" public body which assesses whether convictions or sentences should be referred to a court of appeal. It considers cases in England, Wales and Northern Ireland while a separate commission looks at cases in Scotland. It started work in 1997.

The CCRC has the power to send, or refer, a case back to an appeal court if it considers that there is a real possibility the court will quash the conviction or reduce the sentence in that case.

During the 1970s in particular there were a number of high-profile cases where the convictions were later identified as miscarriages of justice: The Guildford Four, and Judith Ward (1974); The Birmingham Six (1975); and The Maguire Seven (1976). These "shocking" cases, says the CCRC, featured a mixture of false confessions, police misconduct, non-disclosure and issues about the reliability of expert forensic testimony.

"The weaknesses in the criminal justice system exposed by these cases led to the establishment of a Royal Commission on Criminal Justice in 1991," says the CCRC. How slowly do the wheels of justice turn. Its remit included considering whether changes were needed in the arrangements for considering and investigating allegations of miscarriages of justice when appeal rights have been exhausted. This Commission decided that the arrangements for referral of cases back to the courts were incompatible with the constitutional separation of powers between the courts and the executive. So the CCRC was set up, much against the wishes of many in authority who adhered to Lord Denning's view that the imprisonment of innocent people was of no great consequence.

In its "Corporate Plan for 2018-2021", the commission looked back over its 20-year history, noting that: "…the criminal justice system has evolved significantly and the nature of wrongful convictions has therefore, in part at least, changed over time. For example, where in the past the miscarriages of justice we identified often arose from systemic misconduct by investigative authorities, or systemic problems with expert evidence, or from a particular issue, the causes of potential miscarriage now appear to be more diffuse and less easy to identify. Even where the broad cause is the same, such as the failure to disclose material helpful to the defence, its manifestation, and how and where it happens, is very different. The criminal justice system is operated by human beings and occasionally mistakes will be made."

It continued: "The pressures on the criminal justice system remain as intense as ever. Investigative techniques and procedures change and, as they do so, they bring new challenges and opportunities to a criminal justice system that needs to retain the confidence of the public."

It's quite a bold statement from a body which is only supposed to review possible miscarriages of justice. The vision and purpose of the CCRC, as stated in its annual report, are:

- to bring justice to the wrongly convicted by referring cases to the appellate courts;
- to identify, investigate and correct miscarriages of justice in a timely manner; and
- to act independently in the interests of justice and to use our unique knowledge and experience to improve the criminal justice system and inspire confidence in the integrity of the criminal justice process.

That word "integrity" again. Lord Denning would be so proud.

The need for "new evidence", however, still remains, at least partially. The CCRC states: "In order to be able to refer a case to the appeal courts, the Commission generally needs to be able to point to some potentially important new evidence or new legal argument that makes the case look sufficiently different to how it looked at trial or at an earlier appeal. The evidence or argument usually needs to be new in the sense that it was not available at the time of the conviction or the appeal. If the evidence in question was available but not used at the time of the trial or appeal, there will need to be good reasons why it should now be treated as new." So the biggest obstacle to "justice" is still in place.

In 2016-17 the Commission referred 12 cases to the appeal courts: 0.77% of the 1,563 cases concluded that year. In the previous year the referral rate was 1.8% and in 2014-15 it was 2.2%.

In its annual report for 2018-19, it states: "By the end of March 2019, the CCRC had referred 663 cases to the appeal courts at an average rate of around 30 cases per year for 22 years. Those referrals came from 24,078 cases completed by that date. This means that one in every 36 applications to the Commission have been referred for appeal. Of those cases referred, 439 resulted in successful appeals and 200 resulted in appeals dismissed."

The CCRC is funded by the Ministry of Justice; it has a budget of more than £6 million and just over 80 staff, who cost a total of £4.2 million in the 2018-19 financial year.

The Ministry of Justice was established in 2007; up until then matters of "justice" were attended to by the Home Office. It states: "We work to protect and advance the principles of justice. Our vision is to deliver a world-class justice system that works for everyone in society." It has a very long way to go. Despite the oft-repeated statement that justice is blind – blind to wealth, position, colour, etc. – it is still the case that the system substantially favours the wealthy and influential, is still suspicious of race, colour and creed, and falls well short of being impartial and objective and free from political interference.

From the numerous perverse decisions of the Crown Prosecution Service to the mess that is now the government's legal aid system, the entire justice system in the UK – although to a lesser extent in Scotland – is in need of radical overhaul, rather than the tinkering at the edges that has gone on in recent years. It's a battered and broken system – and has been for decades.

In the mid-1970s I had reason to write to the Lord Chancellor about a smallish matter I had been involved with after what I thought had been a hire purchase agreement turned out to be something rather different. Arriving at the court in Kingston upon Thames for the hearing, I was informed it had been postponed. "Shouldn't you have told me about that?" I enquired, having taken time off work to be there. "We can't inform everyone," the lady there told me in a very bored tone. "We will notify you when a new date is set."

"Can I claim the fares for this wasted journey?" I asked. "No!" she said firmly.

Some days later a letter arrived from the court telling me of the outcome of the hearing and the judgment entered. I wrote to ask how this could be and received a reply that the judgment had been entered "in error". A new hearing date was set and a slightly different outcome achieved. The whole court process was a mess. My letter to the Lord Chancellor – who at that time was appointed by the Queen on the advice of the Prime Minister, even though he nominally outranked the PM, so an important figure in the legal system – set out what had happened and the contemptuous, and contemptible, treatment I had received.

The response was hardly surprising: "As the outcome is satisfactory we will not be taking this matter further." In other words, "You are of no account or influence and therefore the court can treat you with utter contempt and we don't care." That must have been the "integrity" that Lord Denning was speaking about. From what people have told me, things haven't changed much.

Sir Patrick Devlin, a Lord of Appeal, lawyer, judge and jurist, said in 1956 that "trial by jury ... is the lamp that shows that freedom lives". But the processes by which a jury is selected leaves much to be desired. My wife did jury service in the 1980s and enjoyed the shambolic experience, so much so that she decided to get more involved in the legal system and became a magistrate, a task with which she became increasingly frustrated because of the way cases were presented. Prosecutors and police witnesses often turned up at court inadequately prepared and many of them clearly held the proceedings in contempt. Voluntary magistrates were often referred to as "wooden-tops" by the more arrogant members of the legal profession – and even by juniors. Eventually she resigned to pursue other interests.

After returning home from open-heart surgery in 2008, my wife received a summons for another spell of jury service. As her convalescence was expected to take at least three months, I responded on her behalf to the Jury Central Summoning Bureau to explain the circumstances and that she would be unable to fulfil this obligation. This brought a response that as she had deferred jury service on an earlier occasion – we had been out of the country – she could not do so again.

Thinking I should enter into the spirit of this, I asked for details of disabled access, etc., at the court in Guildford, Surrey, and how we should deal with any hospital appointments or other medical needs during the period of service. This brought another deadpan response, ignoring all the questions, simply stating that she would be expected at the court on the due date. Then I wrote to say that she would not be there. Finally, someone with an IQ stretching into double figures must have looked at the correspondence and a response came that she would not be required to attend and would henceforth be exempt from jury service. Sense at last. But what a waste of time and money. And hers was not an uncommon experience.

In 1931, Gordon Hewart (later Viscount Hewart), the seventh Lord Chief Justice of England, made legal history when, sitting with two other judges, he quashed a conviction for murder on the grounds that the conviction was not supported by the weight of the evidence. He believed the jury was wrong. If only other judges had been as strong-willed!

Lord Hewart was also the originator of the statement that "not only must justice be done; it must also be seen to be done" or, more correctly, what he actually said was: "... a long line of cases shows that it is not merely of some importance but is of fundamental importance that justice should not only be done, but should manifestly and undoubtedly be seen to be done." Sadly, a great deal of justice in various parts of the UK is meted out behind closed doors – and that is not the way it should be.

Cases of mistaken infallibility

The introduction of automatic teller machines (ATMs) in the late 1960s caused serious problems for quite a few individuals who put their cards in, received no money but had their accounts debited. For some years, people who complained often found themselves being interviewed by the police and in a number of cases charges were laid relating to attempted fraud.

It was a double whammy for these people. The courts often accepted the view of the banks, backed up on no evidence whatsoever by the police, that the machines were "infallible". So people lost their money and gained a criminal record. No doubt there were some genuine attempted frauds but, of course, in the eyes of the judiciary, it is of little consequence if innocent people are convicted.

On one occasion in the 1980s the ATM at Barclays branch in Walton-on-Thames gave me a receipt but no money. I reported this instantly to a non-automated teller inside the bank who took the details and informed me that if the check that evening indicated that the balance in the machine was wrong by the amount I had requested, the money would be returned to my account. A fairly sensible way of handling the matter – one that should have been used in all cases – and I got the money back.

By this time, banks had admitted the machines were not infallible but it is doubtful that any of the wrongful convictions were overturned – such is the integrity of the English justice system. Happily, it is also unlikely, in view of events since, that the police or the courts would in future accept the word of bankers so readily.

Inquest needed into coroners' activities

Coroners are independent judicial officers who investigate deaths reported to them. They are required to make whatever inquiries are necessary to establish the cause or causes of death; this includes ordering a post-mortem examination, obtaining witness statements and medical records, or holding an inquest.

In England and Wales, inquests are the responsibility of a coroner who currently operates under the jurisdiction of the Coroners and Justice Act 2009. Inquests are held into sudden or unexplained deaths and also into the circumstances of discovery of certain valuable artefacts known as "treasure trove". Scotland has a different system: where a sudden, accidental, suspicious, in-custody or unnatural death has occurred, a procurator fiscal investigates the circumstances to determine if the death resulted from natural causes and if not whether a criminal prosecution is warranted or a fatal accident inquiry should be initiated.

The Hillsborough disaster of 15th April 1989, which resulted in the deaths of 96 people with over 760 more injured and many left traumatised, stands as a terrible indictment of not just the English justice system but the "establishment". Government departments, the police, the coroner's court and even some newspapers conspired to give false accounts of what had happened and endeavoured to keep as much as possible under wraps.

In the weeks following the disaster, police and others, including MPs, fed false stories to the press suggesting that hooliganism and drinking by Liverpool supporters were the root causes of the disaster. This blaming of Liverpool fans persisted even after Lord Taylor's Report of 1990 which found that the main cause of the disaster was a failure of control by South Yorkshire Police. Following the Taylor report, the Director of Public Prosecutions ruled there was no evidence to justify prosecution of any individuals or institutions.

The first coroner's inquests into the disaster, completed in 1991, ruled that all the deaths that occurred that day were accidental but the coroner had actually laid down pre-conditions for the inquest that prevented the full truth being established. Families strongly – and naturally – rejected the coroner's findings and continued their fight to have the matter properly investigated. In 1997, Lord Justice Stuart-Smith declared there was no justification for a new inquiry and some private prosecutions brought by the Hillsborough Families Support Group against police officers were unsuccessful.

In 2009, a Hillsborough Independent Panel was formed to review all the evidence. When it reported in 2012, it confirmed the criticisms made by Lord Taylor 19 years earlier while also revealing "new" details about the extent of police efforts to shift blame onto fans – including changing written statements made at the time; the role of other emergency services; and the error of the first inquests. The panel's report resulted in the previous findings of accidental death being quashed and fresh inquests being set up. It also led to two criminal investigations by the police: Operation Resolve to look into the causes of the disaster, and one by the Independent Police Complaints Commission to examine actions by police in the aftermath.

The second inquests opened in April 2014 and lasted just over two years. They ruled that the victims had been unlawfully killed due to grossly negligent failures by police and ambulance services to fulfil their duty of care to the supporters. The inquests also found that the design of the stadium contributed to the crush and that supporters were not to blame for the dangerous conditions.

Shortly afterwards, the then Home Secretary, Theresa May, told the House of Commons: "For 27 years the families and survivors of Hillsborough have fought for justice. They have faced hostility, opposition and obfuscation, and the authorities that should have been trusted have laid blame and tried to protect themselves instead of acting in the public interest." Rarely were truer words spoken in parliament. A proper admission of failure – but only once it had become clear there was no other choice.

Among those guilty of "hostility, opposition and obfuscation" was the Home Office itself, not that this "unfit for purpose" department ever accepted any blame. And even after Mrs May's statement, Andy Burnham, a former Labour MP and Cabinet minister who went on to become Mayor of

Manchester, reported that he had been placed under pressure to stop campaigning on behalf of the people bereaved in the disaster.

In an article for the *Observer*, he described the injustice of Hillsborough as "breathtaking" and "one of the greatest miscarriages of justice in British history". He wrote: "The legal system needs radical change. Its adversarial nature suits the authorities. It can easily intimidate people who are pitched into an intimidating court environment. And the authorities spend public money like water in hiring the best lawyers. By contrast, the victims of any disaster have to scratch around to get whatever legal representation they can. That can't be right."

Margaret Thatcher, Prime Minister at the time of the disaster, was always fulsome in her praise of the police and emergency services and determinedly stuck to the mantra that they had done their best. After Mrs May's statement, John Major, who succeeded Mrs Thatcher as Prime Minister (1990-1997), said, somewhat pathetically, that he wished he had done more while in office … meanwhile Jack Straw, Home Secretary from 1997 to 2001, gave entirely unconvincing accounts of his part in attempting to uncover the truth.

What an indictment of the entire system and, in particular, the failings of coroners' courts, that it should take 27 years to get to the truth of this appalling disaster. Justice? Integrity?

After Mrs May's statement, a journalist at *The Times* at the time of the disaster wrote to his former paper to ask why it had taken 27 years to prove the incompetence by police, emergency services and ground staff that the team of *Times* reporters – and, indeed, those of a number of other national newspapers – had identified within 24 hours of the tragedy. Why indeed!

The 1982 murder in London of the Italian banker, Roberto Calvi, was another case of an absurd decision by a coroner. There were two inquests into Calvi's death: the first, inexplicably, recording a verdict of suicide. After representations by the family, a second inquest was held a year later, when the jury recorded an open verdict, indicating that the court had been unable to determine the exact cause of death. Calvi's family maintained that his death had been a murder. Forensic tests in 1991 indicated, among other things, that Calvi could not have hanged himself but the Home Secretary and the City of London Police dismissed the findings. Their attitude did not change until 2002 when a second report confirmed the details of the first one and in 2007 an Italian court ruled the cause of death was murder.

After the death in July 2003 of David Kelly, a respected authority on biological warfare who had been a UN weapons inspector in Iraq and whose supposedly off-the-record comments had embarrassed the government, the government led by Tony Blair decided to bypass the coroner's court altogether and set up a public inquiry under a known "safe pair of hands", one Lord Hutton, who determined that Dr Kelly had committed suicide; he then ordered all evidence related to the death, including the post-mortem report and photographs of the body, to remain classified for 70 years.

A group of doctors which included a former coroner disputed Lord Hutton's findings and after calls for a full inquest (including one by former Home Secretary Michael Howard), details of the post-mortem were made public in October 2010, reiterating the conclusion of Lord Hutton's report – though serious questions still remain, not least of which is why the normal procedure for a formal inquest was not followed.

Reports of tampering with the system and strange outcomes abound. Justice is certainly not being seen to be done.

In March 2008, for example, it was widely reported that the Ministry of Defence had launched a legal battle to curb coroners' criticisms of the Ministry of Defence at inquests on British troops. This followed verdicts in a coroner's court on deaths of soldiers in Iraq and Afghanistan when the coroner accused the Ministry of "serious failures". The Ministry didn't actually dispute the term "serious failures", it just didn't want them made public as, in the words of one of its legal team, "it could imply a civil legal liability for (a soldier's) death, in breach of the laws governing inquest procedures".

The coroner also criticised "official blunders" and said he faced huge difficulties and frustrations in his efforts to uncover evidence from the MoD.

The MoD was also caught up in inquests into the deaths of four young soldiers at the Princess Royal Barracks in Deepcut, Surrey, between 1995 and 2002, all of whom had suffered gunshot wounds. This is yet another tragic tale of officialdom covering its tracks, with matters dragging on and on and on and no satisfactory conclusion for the families of the soldiers involved.

Justice? Integrity? Action? None of the above.

Not much in the way of justice for sexual abuse victims

And what about the young victims of sexual abuse? Instances were being reported as far back as the 1970s and 80s but the police, the government, the churches, schools and children's homes involved all managed to either ignore them or sweep them under the carpet.

It isn't just a British problem. In Ireland, for example, the police, government and the Roman Catholic church took no action other than to subject victims to even more cruelty in case the image of the church was damaged. Many other countries have had similar issues. In Britain, however, it was virtually impossible for victims to get their voices heard as the establishment closed ranks.

Finally, the Home Office set up an "independent" inquiry but, as might be expected, the department made a complete hash of it; by 2018 the enquiry had its fourth head and had made remarkably little progress. The inquiry's website states: "The Independent Inquiry into Child Sexual Abuse was set up because of serious concerns that some organisations had failed and were continuing to fail to protect children from sexual abuse. Our remit is huge, but as a statutory inquiry we have unique authority to address issues that have persisted despite previous inquiries and attempts at reform."

"Serious concerns that some organisations had failed"! Everyone knows that numerous organisations have failed miserably and tolerated disgusting practices by their staff. This is vastly more than just "serious concerns". Get a grip!

Will, or can, any of the victims ever get or expect justice? Some in America have received payouts from the Roman Catholic church in exchange for taking no further action and clergy involved have sometimes been moved into jobs where they have less contact with youngsters. But why are the clergy there and here not treated as people are in other fields? Why are they not tried and imprisoned? Why are many still active in churches and schools and children's homes? Where is the justice the victims have a right to expect?

Other areas of the justice system are also clearly in need of overhaul. In August 2018, the Ministry of Justice had to "step in" (as they called it) to take control of a privately-run prison in Birmingham which, it was reported, had been "dogged by soaring violence, drug use and appalling living conditions" and where there were serious concerns over safety, security and decency. The prisons watchdog had graded the jail as "poor" in every category. It was not the only prison where problems were occurring.

The probation service is also not working as it should. Attempts to privatise it, despite warnings that it wouldn't work, failed miserably – and expensively.

In June 2015, the then new Justice Secretary, Michael Gove, said that while those with money can secure the finest legal provision in the world, "the reality in our courts for many of our citizens is that the justice system is failing them badly," and he went on to describe the justice system as "creaking and outdated". The human cost of failings by the legal system is, he said, unforgivable.

And let's not get started on the police, whose many failings have been well-documented elsewhere. As in any field of endeavour, most are decent, hard-working people but funding and other constraints – not least a misguided notion of political correctness – have led to a plethora of problems.

In 2018, the book *The Secret Barrister: Stories of the Law and How it is Broken* – a critical first-hand account of the current state of the criminal justice system in England and Wales by an anonymous author known only as The Secret Barrister – was described by one reviewer as "a plea to rescue a justice system that has become utterly broken" and which "leaves some of the most vulnerable people at the mercy of a system that is designed to be incomprehensible to even the most highly educated lay person".

Basically, much of the system stinks – but don't expect meaningful reform any time soon. As for integrity, you can find it in a dictionary but there is not much of it in the British system of justice. Yes, the British system is preferable to many in the wider world, but that is no reason to allow its shocking decline to continue.

Racism, bigotry and hate crime

Why can't people tolerate each other?

Very few days pass without reports in newspapers and on radio and television about racist behaviour in the UK – whether at football matches or on the streets or elsewhere. Racial and religious intolerance show no signs of decreasing. The ability to put racist comments and even death threats anonymously on some social media platforms has certainly exacerbated the problem, giving bigots, weirdos and the lunatic fringe an open forum to spout vitriol and bile with little danger of being called to account.

The UK used to have a Commission for Racial Equality, a non-departmental public body which aimed to address racial discrimination and promote racial equality. This was replaced in 2006 by the Equality and Human Rights Commission, also a non-departmental public body, which aims to "promote and uphold equality and human rights ideals and laws across England, Scotland and Wales".

The commission states on its website that its role and purpose is to "stand up for freedom, compassion and justice in changing times. Our work is driven by a simple belief, if everyone gets a fair chance in life, we all thrive". These are fine-sounding words but, as the 17th century "proverb" (origin unknown) states, "Fine words butter no parsnips" – meaning that nothing concrete is achieved by empty words. Sadly, most of the evidence currently points to very little having been achieved, especially in the field of racial harmony.

The Monitoring Group, set up in Southall, West London, in 1981 by community campaigners and lawyers who sought to challenge the growth of racism in the locality, has gradually developed into an anti-racist charity working throughout the nation. It describes itself as the "leading exponent of family-led empowerment and justice campaigns in the UK".

This group took part in a parliamentary round-table on racism and hate crime in April 2018, which noted the increases, often dramatic and dangerous, in hate crimes, with violent hate crimes continuing to form the overwhelming majority of hate crimes reported to the police – more than 80,000 in 2016-17, nearly 30% up on the previous year.

It also stated, not entirely accurately, that the Brexit campaign had been wholly anti-immigrant in nature and fuelled by xenophobia and racism, consolidating far-right thinking in mainstream British politics.

109

In 2017, the National Centre for Social Research (NatCen), which conducts the annual British Social Attitudes Survey, said that one in four people in Britain admitted to being prejudiced towards people of other races, with 26% saying they were "very" or "a little" prejudiced towards them.

The proportion saying they are racially prejudiced has never fallen below a quarter when people are asked the same question in the survey – which began in 1983. It peaked at 39% in 1987 and in 2011 was at 37%.

In each survey, 3,000 people are asked various questions relating to what it's like to live in Britain and how they think Britain is run. NatCen says the people who participate are chosen using a "random probability sampling" technique and the results "are representative" of the British population – a somewhat unlikely claim but nevertheless it is probably a not unreasonable assessment of trends.

The 2017 report also indicated that: men (29%) were more likely than women (23%) to say they were racially prejudiced; 33% of Conservative party supporters described themselves as racially prejudiced, compared to 18% of Labour supporters (an interesting finding considering claims of antisemitism in the latter – of which more later); 34% of people who voted Leave in the 2016 referendum on the EU described themselves as racially prejudiced while just 18% of Remain voters described themselves in this way.

A spokesperson for NatCen said the numbers provided clear evidence that a significant minority of people in Britain feel prejudiced towards people of other races. "Prejudice on this scale is something we as a society should be concerned about, not least as there is a significant body of evidence that even subtle racial prejudices contribute to racial inequality in areas such as education, employment and in the criminal justice system," she said.

A European Social Survey carried out in 2014 showed that almost one in five Britons (18%) agreed that "some races or ethnic groups are born less intelligent" and 44% said that some are naturally harder working. Amazing. But these views persist.

And in February 2020, the Archbishop of Canterbury, Justin Welby (a "Most Reverend") told a meeting of the General Synod in London that the Church of England was "deeply and institutionally racist" and declared that he was "ashamed of our history and our failure".

The term "institutional racism" appears to have been first used in 1967 by Stokely Carmichael (later known as Kwame Ture) and Charles V. Hamilton in *Black Power: The Politics of Liberation.*

It was defined in the UK by Sir William Macpherson in the 1999 report into the murder of a black teenager, Stephen Lawrence, as: "The collective failure of an organisation to provide an appropriate and professional service to people because of their colour, culture, or ethnic origin. It can be seen or detected in processes, attitudes and behaviour which amount to discrimination through unwitting prejudice, ignorance, thoughtlessness and racist stereotyping which disadvantage minority ethnic people." He was referring to the Metropolitan Police Service in London.

Since then the term has been applied, sometimes without just cause, to many organisations and institutions in the UK, including the Home Office – though certainly with good reason in the case of that very troubled department. It has, however, become debased through overuse, in the same way that the term "zero tolerance" (which first appeared in the USA in the 1960s, moving to the UK several decades later) has lost its impact.

One form of racial and religious bigotry that has been much in the news is "antisemitism". As reports have been concerned particularly – but not exclusively – with the Labour Party, it's worth a closer look, and most of the rest of this chapter will be devoted to it.

What does the term mean? For most people nowadays it refers to the abuse of Jewish people. The Jews have been a much abused and mistreated race for many hundreds of years and the subject of much irrational hatred. Antisemitism, however, is an inappropriate term for the harassment, and worse, of Jewish people in the UK and many other countries.

In historical terms, Jews, Palestinians and Arabs are all "semites" (or "shemites") – Semitic people – although the term "anti-Semite" (or "antisemitism") is now, for some obscure reason, used only to refer to Jews, with the older meaning of semite now either forgotten or ignored.

According to an authoritative article in *Encyclopaedia Britannica*, members of the Semitic group are spread throughout North Africa and south-west Asia and have played pre-eminent roles in the linguistic and cultural landscape of the Middle East for more than 4,000 years.

"In the early 21st century," the article continues, "the most important Semitic language, in terms of the number of speakers, was Arabic. Standard Arabic is spoken as a first language by more than 200 million people living in a broad area stretching from the Atlantic coast of northern Africa to western Iran; an additional 250 million people in the region speak Standard Arabic as a secondary language."

So, Semitic people were, simply, those who spoke the Semitic languages. The word was derived from Shem (hence "shemites"), one of the three sons of Noah mentioned in the Old Testament book of Genesis.

So why not simply use the term "anti-Jewish" to cover the irrational hatred of this race? It would make much more sense than antisemitism.

In a booklet called *Hate Crime Operational Guidance*, the College of Policing, described as the professional body for policing in the UK, says that "antisemitism is a historic and deeply rooted prejudice which continues to affect communities".

In a section headed "Race hate crime", antisemitism is taken to be a combination of race hate crimes where the hostility is targeted towards Jewish people or communities and religious hate crime targeted towards Judaism.

It continues: "Jewish people are accepted in UK courts to be an ethnic group. Victims may, therefore, perceive crimes targeting Jewish people to be either a religious hate crime or a racist crime, even when the victim is secular or does not have links with Israel. Antisemitic hate crime takes place where a recordable crime is committed and the victim perceives it is motivated (wholly or partially) by antisemitic hostility. Jewish people may report such crimes as racially or religiously motivated, even when the victim is secular or does not have links with Israel."

According to the Campaign Against Antisemitism, the international definition of antisemitism is: "A certain perception of Jews, which may be expressed as hatred toward Jews. Rhetorical and physical manifestations of antisemitism are directed toward Jewish or non-Jewish individuals and/or their property, toward Jewish community institutions and religious facilities." Intriguingly, the "non-Jewish individuals and property" are not specified.

Campaign Against Antisemitism is "a volunteer-led charity dedicated to exposing and countering antisemitism through education and zero-tolerance enforcement of the law". It was established in August 2014 by members of the Anglo-Jewish community in the UK, so it is perhaps not surprising that it limits the scope of the word "semites" to Jews. It says: "We work closely with police forces around the country, the Crown Prosecution Service, regulatory bodies and the government to ensure that antisemitism is detected, investigated and punished with the full force of the law. We focus on criminal antisemitism and antisemitic acts committed by professionals or institutions which are subject to special regulation, such as lawyers, teachers, sportspeople and charities. We also provide training and advice to the authorities, whilst also scrutinising their performance and holding them to account when they fall short."

It adds (on its website): "Working closely with senior journalists and advertising professionals, we run proactive campaigns to ensure that the public is aware of anti-Jewish racism and the immense societal danger that it poses."

The definition of antisemitism has, however, been adopted in the UK by, among others, the government, the London Assembly, the Greater Manchester Combined Authority, the College of Policing and the National Union of Students. Internationally it has been adopted by, among others, the governments of Israel, Austria, Bulgaria, Germany, Lithuania, Macedonia and Romania, the European Parliament, the US Senate and Department of State and the International Holocaust Remembrance Alliance.

In 2005, the EU Monitoring Centre on Racism and Xenophobia (EUMC), now the EU Agency for Fundamental Rights (FRA), adopted a "working definition of antisemitism" which has become a standard definition used around the world. In 2016, the House of Commons Home Affairs Committee joined Campaign Against Antisemitism's long-standing call for the British government and its agencies, as well as all political parties, to formally adopt the International Definition of Antisemitism, following which the British government did so.

The *Oxford Compact English Dictionary* defines "semite" as "a member of people speaking a Semitic language, in particular the Jews and Arabs". Trust the good old *Oxford Dictionary* to get it right, apart from leaving out the Palestinians. But under "anti-Semitism" it puts: "hostility to or prejudice against Jews". Nothing more than that. Muddled thinking.

Back to *Encyclopaedia Britannica*. "Anti-Semitism, hostility toward or discrimination against Jews as a religious or racial group. The term anti-Semitism was coined in 1879 by the German agitator Wilhelm Marr to designate the anti-Jewish campaigns under way in central Europe at that time. Although the term now has wide currency, it is a misnomer, since it implies a discrimination against all Semites."

Clarity at last. Why do we not call anti-Jewish acts and words anti-Jewish acts and words and stop calling it "antisemitism" or "anti-Semitism", for that is not a suitable name for the hatred of Jews. We are being asked to refer to a centuries-old problem with a relatively recent and misleading term.

Could we not have some rational thinking and discussion about the entirely irrational and abominable hatred of this hugely and appallingly, violently mistreated and abused race? And, clearly, "anti-Jewish" should not be confused with being anti-Zionist or anti-Israel.

Interestingly, Jordan is known officially as the Hashemite Kingdom of Jordan, with dear old Shem right there in the middle. Arabs make up the bulk of the population, alongside Bedouin (nomadic Arabs or desert dwellers), Palestinian and other ethnic groups. A fine bunch of semites or shemites – but no one is supposed to mention that.

Racism and bigotry are complicated issues and are unlikely to disappear. It might help, however, if there were more informed discussions, less muddled thinking and clear terminology – plus a dramatic change of heart in those who harbour such irrational hatreds. We can only hope.

One last thing. In December 2019, the Prime Minister of Israel, Benjamin Netanyahu, accused the International Criminal Court of being anti-semitic when it announced its intention to pursue a war crimes probe into Israel's actions in the Palestinian territories. Even in this Humpty Dumpty era (see "Starting point" at the beginning of this book), can the abuse of one semitic race by another semitic race really be considered anti-semitic?

Politics – 1

The worldwide leadership conundrum

"The longer I stay in power, the better I get at ruling," said Angela Merkel, while in the process of seeking a fourth term of office at the age of 63 after 12 years as Chancellor of Germany. Asked by readers of the German newspaper *Bild* in August 2017 whether she had learned from the demise of Chancellor Helmut Kohl who served for 16 years but saw his popularity drop sharply during his final term, she replied: "I do not make historical comparisons." To the question, "Do you believe you get better the longer you govern?" she stated, "Yes – a clear question, a clear answer."

Her fourth campaign was, unfortunately for her, not an unqualified success as voters did not support her as much as she had hoped. Nevertheless, she clung on to power, rather like the UK's Theresa May, who refused to budge after a much shorter period in office.

A look back over national leaders – heads of state (other than those such as the Queen who fulfil mainly ceremonial or limited constitutional duties) and prime ministers or chancellors or whatever title they might have – shows that few achieve anything positive for the welfare of their citizens after they have served about seven years in office but in many, far too many, cases their own (and their families') wealth and welfare improve considerably.

Many, sadly, reach their "best before" date well before seven years in power; very, very few reach it after that time. Indeed, the usual time taken for leaders in most parts of the world to reach their "best (or better) before" date is about 6.5 years. Margaret Thatcher and Tony Blair certainly did.

One of the great strengths of American politics is that presidents serve for a maximum of eight years, the eighth year generally being with "lame duck" status when little is achieved, apart from bestowing favours on friends. If only all countries stuck to similar rules. How sad it is for nations when leaders amend their constitutions to allow them to stay in office for longer. There is not the remotest possibility that they will serve well in that extra time.

China did it early in 2018 to allow President Xi Jinping, in office since 2012, to carry on beyond the previous 10-year limit; President Recep Tayyip Erdogan of Turkey, who took office in 2014 having been Prime Minister from 2003, pushed through changes to allow himself to become head of state and head of government almost indefinitely; Fidel Castro led Cuba as Prime

Minister from 1959 and in 1976 combined the roles of PM and President to give himself absolute power until ill-health caused him to slip into the background in 2006; and the list goes on.

Smaller (by population) countries have been doing it too. In Turkmenistan, for instance, a country with fewer than six million people, the President, Gurbanguly Berdimuhamedow, took office in 2006 and headed a committee in 2017 which increased the presidential term from five to seven years and removed age limits for candidates so he could carry on for the rest of his life if he wished. He has allowed no meaningful opposition and, according to Human Rights Watch (the authoritative non-governmental human rights organisation set up in 1978), he and his relatives and associates have unlimited power and total control over all aspects of public life, including the media.

Angela Merkel, who was described at various times as the *de facto* leader of the European Union, the most powerful woman in the world and the leader of the Free World, once said: "Whoever decides to dedicate their life to politics knows that earning money isn't the top priority." But take a look at leaders past and present across Africa, Asia, Central and South America and the Middle East – and elsewhere – and you begin to wonder. It seems that the longer they remain in power, the greater the wealth they accumulate.

A few examples among many…

• Ferdinand Marcos came to power in the Philippines at the end of 1965 and ruled until 1986. His later years in power were marked by rampant government corruption and economic stagnation – with the rich getting richer and the poor poorer. One historian refers to his period in power as featuring "a spectacular level of corruption and looting of the national treasury". Backed by successive US administrations, he scrapped the country's constitution in 1973 and introduced one giving himself sweeping new powers. This stayed in place until his fall from power in 1986. Marcos, his family and his close associates looted the Philippines' economy of billions of dollars through embezzlements and other corrupt practices and, when he died in Hawaii in 1989, he was an extremely rich man with a substantial property portfolio in several countries.

• Mobutu Sese Seko, the military officer who dominated the vast Democratic Republic of Congo (formerly the Belgian Congo which Mobutu renamed Zaire) in central Africa for three decades, achieved power with military backing and succeeded in staying there with help from the USA – via the CIA which had helped engineer the overthrow of the democratically elected leadership – along with, mainly, Belgium,

116

France and Britain and, later, China. In January 1972 he changed his name from Joseph-Désiré Mobutu to Mobutu Sese Seko Koko Ngbendu Wa Za Banga, meaning, "The all-powerful warrior who, because of his endurance and inflexible will to win, will go from conquest to conquest, leaving fire in his wake." He amassed an enormous personal fortune through economic exploitation, corruption and embezzlement, earning a reputation as one of the world's foremost exemplars of kleptocracy and nepotism. He would, for instance, hire an Air France Concorde for family shopping expeditions to Paris or for such things as dental treatment in the south of France, where he owned a chateau. He ruled from 1965 until 1997 and died soon after his ousting from power as one of the world's wealthiest men.

• President Dos Santos stepped down as President of Angola in August 2017 after 38 years in the post – because of worsening health. He remained, however, as head of the People's Movement for the Liberation in Angola and had pushed a law through parliament the previous month to block the new President from removing the heads of the army, police and intelligence services for eight years. His daughter was said at the time to be Africa's richest woman and was in charge of the state oil company while his son headed a sovereign wealth fund. One commentator said Mr Dos Santos was "closing the doors but taking the keys" as his time of running an appallingly repressive government came to an end. Before agreeing to step aside, he made sure he obtained guarantees of permanent immunity from prosecution for any crimes committed during his time in office: he had gained an international reputation as one of Africa's most zealous kleptocrats, using his position to enrich himself and his extended family.

• In 2016-17, President Robert Mugabe of Zimbabwe reportedly spent £39 million on travelling abroad, much of it for hospital treatment in Singapore. The sum was more than twice that spent on improving hospitals in Zimbabwe during the same period. He became President in 1987 after having been Prime Minister since 1980 and, despite being responsible for the economic ruination of much of the country and many thousands of deaths, he said at the age of 93 that he wanted to "compete" in another election and live to 100. His wife Grace said that if he died before the election he should run as a corpse. He was, however, ousted from power in 2017, although he was allowed to retain the wealth and homes he had gained during his rule: his personal fortune was reliably estimated at around £1 billion, much of it invested outside Zimbabwe. The home he shared with his wife in Harare has been described as "extraordinarily opulent"; other assets, some of which were shared with Mrs Mugabe, included bank accounts in Switzerland, the Channel Islands and the Bahamas along with properties in South Africa, Malaysia and Singapore and even in Scotland, as well as 14 farms in Zimbabwe including one of the largest dairy farms in southern Africa. Mr Mugabe received an honorary knighthood from the Queen in 1994, though this was annulled in 2008, well into his reign of terror and economic mismanagement. He died in September 2019.

• Demonstrating that size doesn't matter as far as kleptocracy is concerned, President Teodora Obiang has ruled Equatorial Guinea, with its population of about 720,000, since 1979, and he and his family have amassed substantial fortunes. Human Rights Watch stated in 2016 that, "Vast oil revenues fund lavish lifestyles for the small elite surrounding the president while a large proportion of the population lives in poverty." The president and his son, who also happens to be a vice-president, spend considerable sums on mansions, cars, art – and Michael Jackson memorabilia. At one point, the son owned a house in Paris worth close to £100 million. They survived a coup in 2004 which was reported to be part-funded by Margaret Thatcher's son Mark.

• Alberto Fujimori was President of Peru from 1990 to 2000. He tendered his presidential resignation by fax from Japan after fleeing Peru on an aircraft loaded with bullion and diamonds in the midst of a corruption scandal and accusations of human rights violations and crimes against humanity (he was implicated in Peru's death squads which were responsible for the disappearance of more than 4,000 people). The money he made from embezzlement was believed to total about £1.4 billion. Transparency International* considered the money embezzled by Fujimori to be the seventh most for a head of government active between 1984 and 2004. [* This is an organisation active in more than 100 countries which has the vision of: "a world in which government politics, business, civil society and the daily lives of people are free of corruption". It has an international secretariat in Berlin and states: "We work together with governments, businesses and citizens to stop the abuse of power, bribery and secret deals."]

• Zine el-Abidine Ben Ali, President of Tunisia from 1987 to 2011, fled the country in January 2011 with millions of dollars in gold and assets on his aircraft. He was the only presidential candidate in 1994, winning 99.9% of the vote, while in 1999 he received 99.44%. In 2002 he amended the country's constitution to allow a president to stay in power until the age of 75 and to be re-elected an unlimited number of times. His regime was widely considered to be one of the Arab world's most repressive regimes – a staggering claim when you look at other governments in the region including the appallingly repressive and corrupt monarchies. When he was ousted, he took refuge in Saudi Arabia, which refused to allow his extradition. Ben Ali and his family had built a fortune worth billions of dollars by illegally appropriating national assets and skimming wealth from most sectors of the Tunisian economy. In June 2011 a Tunisian court convicted Ben Ali and his wife Leila Trabelsi in absentia of having embezzled public funds and sentenced them to 35 years in prison. The trial focused on large quantities of cash and jewels found in one of Ben Ali's palaces. In a second trial soon after, he was convicted of smuggling drugs, guns and archaeological objects and sentenced to 15 years in prison, but he remained free up until his death in 2019.

• Nicolae Ceauşescu was President of Romania from 1974 until he was overthrown and executed in a revolution in December 1989. Another tyrant honoured by the Queen (in 1978), his knighthood was revoked on the day before his execution. Ceauşescu's megalomania and self-aggrandisement are legendary and he created a bizarre cult of personality. He made his wife Elena the Deputy Prime Minister and ruled Romania according to orthodox Communist principles, causing food shortages by forcing the export of most of the country's agricultural products. His rule included mass surveillance of his citizens and violent reprisals against any dissent. As Romania plunged into mass poverty under his draconian austerity programme, he continued to be fêted the world over. He ordered the construction of a palace in the centre of Bucharest which would be a home for himself and Elena as well as being the location of the Romanian Parliament. The colossal structure took 13 years to build, is incredibly ornate, and is the second largest administrative building in the world after The Pentagon. It has a height of 84 metres, an area of 365,000 square metres and is claimed to be the heaviest building in the world. Its 23 sections contain the two houses of the parliament along with three museums and an international conference centre. In 1990, media magnate Rupert Murdoch tried to buy the building for $US1 billion dollars but his bid was rejected. Prince Charles owns a number of properties in the Transylvanian part of Romania and can claim distant kinship with Vlad "The Impaler" Tepes, the 15th-century Wallachian ruler on whom the Irish novelist Bram Stoker based Dracula.

• Jean-Claude (Baby Doc) Duvalier succeeded his father as President of Haiti in 1971 at the age of 19 and stayed in power until he was kicked out in 1986, whereupon he fled to France with millions of pounds he had embezzled from the severely impoverished country. Thousands of Haitians were killed or tortured and hundreds of thousands fled the country during his presidency. He maintained a remarkably lavish lifestyle (his state-sponsored wedding in 1980 cost about US$3 million) while poverty was said to be the most widespread of any country in the Western Hemisphere. The country's constitution gave him near-absolute power and opposition was not tolerated. Much of the Duvaliers' wealth came from the Régie du Tabac (Tobacco Administration), a tobacco monopoly which Baby Doc expanded to include the proceeds from other government enterprises.

The list goes on and on. Further in the past we had figures such as Rafael Trujillo, the brutal dictator of the Dominican Republic from 1930 to 1961. His "reign" has been described as one of the longest, cruellest and most absolute in modern times. He had total control of the military, appointed family members to key offices, strictly enforced censorship and conformity laws, and ordered the murder of political opponents and the massacre of thousands of Haitian immigrants. He also managed to dominate the church hierarchy, educational system, entertainment industry, and virtually every other element of Dominican society, amassing a vast fortune for himself by taking ownership of virtually everything he wanted – including land, airlines, trading monopolies, manufacturers and most sugar cane producers – amounting to about three-fifths of the nation's gross domestic product and workforce. And his rule overlapped with some of the vilest, cruellest dictators, particularly in Germany and Russia, that the world has known.

Not every dictator in history was in it for the money. Examples…

• Augusto Pinochet, President of Chile from 1973 to 1990, ran a military dictatorship and crushed all political opposition through mass arrests, summary trials, systematic torture – it is estimated that well over 30,000 people were tortured – and "disappearances", with more than 2,000 executions. He introduced the "Caravan of Death", an army unit that travelled the country by helicopter, murdering and torturing his opponents. Opponents who went into exile were hunted down by Pinochet's intelligence agencies. Rather strangely, Margaret Thatcher, when Prime Minister of the UK, expressed her support and admiration for him – something she said she was proud of.

• Pol Pot, whose real name was Saloth Sar, ruled "Democratic Kampuchea", now Cambodia, from 1975 until 1979. From the start, he set about destroying his own people. During his four years at the head of the Khmer Rouge regime, about three million people – a quarter of the country's population – were brutally murdered. His targets covered everyone considered "potentially dangerous", which included the military, specialists of all kinds, including teachers and doctors, officials and educated people in general. Education and religion were abolished and schools were turned into prisons or torture sites.

• Enver Hoxha ruled Albania for 40 years after the end of World War II, first as Prime Minister and from 1954 as supreme leader until his death in 1985. He achieved a great deal for the country with electricity being connected to every rural district, disease epidemics stamped out, and illiteracy drastically reduced. But ... he resorted to brutal Stalinist tactics and, according to *Encyclopaedia Britannica*, his government imprisoned, executed or exiled thousands of landowners, Muslim and Christian clerics, peasants who resisted collectivisation, and disloyal party officials. Private property was confiscated by the state; all churches, mosques and other religious institutions were closed; and all cultural and intellectual endeavours were put at the service of socialism and the state.

This list too could go on and on.

Nowadays we have the appalling non-royal dynasties in places such as Syria and North Korea, and royal ones in Saudi Arabia, Bahrain and elsewhere. While the Syrian and North Korean leaders revel in a lifestyle that few of their citizens enjoy, many royals, almost all of them fabulously wealthy, plunder their nations' wealth and grow even richer, and a number still maintain absolute control.

The French philosopher and diplomat, Joseph de Maistre (1753-1821), once said: "Every nation gets the government it deserves." Can that really be true? Do nations truly deserve the dreadful governments, whether led by monarchs or "commoners", we have had in much of the world for the last 70 or so years: the corrupt, repressive, domineering, self-serving, money-grabbing heads of state and government who have amassed vast fortunes while their citizens suffer deprivations ranging from severe to extreme? Do people in nations where they have no say in who governs or rules them really deserve the appalling treatment meted out to them?

There is a brilliant, poignant poem titled *Pity The Nation*, written in 2007 by Lawrence Ferlinghetti of San Francisco, who turned 100 in March 2019, which should be read by everyone, leaders and led. It can be found on numerous websites and is read by Mr Ferlinghetti himself on https://voxpopulisphere.com/2017/07/30/video-lawrence-ferlinghetti-reads-pity-the-nation/.

It is amazingly relevant in the era of Donald Trump and Boris Johnson, Vladimir Putin and Xi Jinping, Kim Jong-un and dozens of others, and begins: *Pity the nation whose people are sheep, and whose shepherds mislead them, Pity the nation whose leaders are liars, whose sages are silenced, and whose bigots haunt the airwaves.* Well worth a listen and a ponder.

There's more to leadership than leading

North Korea's leaders, the Kim dynasty, have tended to be reclusive, keeping their private lives very much to themselves. It wouldn't do if their subjects knew how well their rulers were living while they themselves struggled to survive. But Kim Jong-il, successor to Kim Il-Sung and father of Kim Jong-un, who ruled, brutally, from 1994 until 2011, didn't mind some things about himself being known. The state newspaper, *Rodong Sinmun*, once reported that the person known as Dear Leader was "an outstanding great master of witty remarks as well as the greatest man ever known in history". He composed six operas "better than all the operas mankind has ever created" and in his first attempt at golf he scored five holes in one and beat the world record for a single round by 25 strokes. Among his other talents, he could summon rain at will and he showed "wonderful skill at making rice cakes". Not bad for the lad described after his death by the BBC's John Simpson as "running the country as if he owned it". He is believed to have amassed a fortune running into several billion dollars, most of which passed into the hands of Kim Jong-un.

The world's royals – an extraordinarily wealthy bunch

There are currently more than two dozen monarchies in the world, with kings, queens, sultans, emperors and emirs (or amirs) ruling or reigning over a total of 43 countries. There are 16 countries where the people are, technically at least, subjects of the British monarchy. Two monarchs, in Malaysia and the

Vatican (the Pope is technically a monarch), are "elected". Many of the monarchs still wield considerable power while a number have absolute power; others, like the British monarchy, reign rather than rule though even constitutional monarchies can still have considerable influence.

One thing they nearly all have in common is their fabulous wealth. Here's a brief look at some of them…

• Saudi Arabia is an absolute monarchy and the leader is both King and Prime Minister as well as head of the House of Saud. When King Abdullah bin Abdulaziz died in January 2015 at the age of 90 after a reign of just under 10 years, the British Prime Minister, David Cameron, said he was deeply saddened and stated: "He will be remembered for his long years of service to the kingdom, for his commitment to peace and for strengthening understanding between faiths." It's hard to believe that a British Prime Minister could utter such nonsense. Human rights campaigners were outraged by the adulation paid to this brutal, despotic ruler. The King's successor, the ageing Salman bin Abdulaziz Al Saud, is believed to have a personal net fortune of more than $US18 billion and the Saudi royal family is believed to be the world's richest. Prince Charles counts the Saudi royals as his friends and has been a regular visitor there, giving truth to Aesop's words: "A man is known by the company he keeps" (an expression coined around 600 BC). One of the most tongue-in-cheek (or maybe plain absurd) letters spotted in a British newspaper was on 25th January 2004 when the ambassador of the Royal Embassy of Saudi Arabia wrote to the *Sunday Times* to object to the paper's description of his country as a "despotic state". "We are neither cruel nor oppressive," he wrote, adding that "torture is against the law". That must have been a comfort to the victims. Crown Prince Mohammed bin Salman, son of the current King, has been projecting himself as a reformer but he gives every appearance of being as cruel and despotic as his predecessors. The brutal killing of Jamal Khashoggi, a journalist frequently described as a Saudi dissident, in the Saudi consulate in Istanbul in October 2018 hardly enhanced his reputation.

• Sheikh Sabah Ahmed al-Sabah is the 15th ruler and 5th Emir of Kuwait; born in 1929, he took office in 2006. He is head of the royal family which has been in power in some form since the early 1700s. It is an offence to criticise him and in May 2016 six people, including three from the royal family, were jailed for just such an offence. He is estimated to be worth a mere $US400 million although he is said to own

4.4 million of the 7 million acres that make up Kuwait. Part of the land he does not own is the American military property that houses the largest American military base in the Middle East.

• Sheikh Tamim bin Hamad Al Thani is the current Amir of Qatar, having taken office in June 2013 after his father's abdication. The al-Thani family, which has ruled Qatar since 1825, is known for ostentatious wealth and for working aggressively to expand their oil-funded influence. The family, which controls the Qatar Investment Fund, has massive holdings in London and the UK, including Harrods, 95% of the 87-storey Shard, 8% of the London Stock Exchange, nearly 7% of Barclays Bank, the Olympic Village, half of One Hyde Park (believed to be the world's most expensive apartment block), plus the site of Chelsea Barracks and the former US embassy building in Grosvenor Square, along with an estimated £200 million "palace" in Regent's Park. In August 2018 the Qatari royals put their personalised Boeing 747-8 up for sale – at around $US500 million; it has 10 bathrooms, several lounges spread over two floors, a lavish bedroom suite, a medical centre and a dining room which doubles up as a boardroom. Qatar, which is about the size of Yorkshire, was a British protectorate from 1916 to 1971. Strictly speaking, the Amir actually owns the entire country.

• Sheikh Khalifa bin Zayed bin Sultan Al Nahyan is the Emir of Abu Dhabi as well as President of the United Arab Emirates, He came to power in 2004 although as Crown Prince he had been acting as President since the late 1990s. The sheikh is also chairman of Abu Dhabi Investment Authority, which manages $US875 billion in assets, the largest amount managed by a nation's head of state in the world. The Al Nahyans' family fortune is believed to be in the region of $US150 billion, with the sheikh himself being worth some $US5 billion.

• Hamad ibn Isa Al Khalifa is the King of Bahrain, acting as monarch and head of state. In February 2002, the then Emir declared that Bahrain was a kingdom and made himself the first king. The al-Khalifa family, which is Sunni, has ruled over this small island nation, with its Shiite majority, since 1783. Though the so-called constitutional monarchy grants Shiites some role in the government, it's little more than a token gesture and when pro-democracy riots began in 2011 they were brutally crushed and their leaders were imprisoned, along with doctors who had treated injured demonstrators. In 2015, the leader of the constitutional opposition was jailed for four years after being accused of plotting to overthrow the monarchy, inciting sectarianism and inciting others to break the law. He was acquitted of the first charge, but convicted of the others. His real "crimes" were to boycott what he called sham elections and to call for political reform. The Americans, who usually care little for how regimes treat their subjects as long as they remain friendly to the US, took what was described as "a robustly critical view", especially after their assistant secretary of state was expelled from the country for meeting opposition leaders. A spokesperson for the UK government, however, made it clear that Britain was standing behind Bahrain and said it was "travelling in the right direction" – an obviously ludicrous claim. But the King, as well as the Crown Prince, have a close relationship with Britain's royal family – he was seated in the royal box close to the Queen at her 90th birthday celebrations at Windsor in 2016. Both the King and the Crown Prince own enormous yachts and the King's net worth has been estimated at around $US5 billion. Not bad for a country occupying less than 300 square miles and with a population of just 1.4 million. Bahraini journalists risk five-year prison terms for offences which include "undermining" the government and religion and some well-known journalists and bloggers have been put behind bars. Journalists were also targeted by officials during the anti-government protests in 2011. In 2014, Reporters Without Borders (RSF) described Bahrain as the "kingdom of disinformation" and added Bahrain to its list of "Enemies of the Internet".

• Swaziland is another absolute monarchy, having been led by King Mswati III since 1986, when he was barely 18 years old. The country was renamed by the King as the Kingdom of eSwatini in April 2018. This landlocked nation in Southern Africa occupies about 6,000 square miles and has a population of 1.23 million. National law states that the throne is the sole landowner in the entire country. The King is believed to have 15 wives and 24 children, but can only marry once his brides-to-be are pregnant to prove they can produce heirs. He is estimated to be worth about $US200 million, making him the third richest king in Africa, and has a passion for luxury cars. Because of negative reports over his car collections, he banned people from taking photographs of them. He attended Queen Elizabeth's diamond jubilee celebrations at Windsor in 2012 and was greeted by human rights campaigners who

125

criticised the lavish lifestyle he led while people in his country were suffering from starvation. He also attended Prince William's wedding.

• Hassanal Bolkiah has been Brunei's Sultan – absolute monarch – and Prime Minister since 1967, and he appoints virtually all of Brunei's ruling bodies, including the Legislative Council and the Supreme and Sharia Courts. His 1,800-room palace, the Istana Nurul Iman, is considered the world's largest private residence. He was once regarded as the world's richest man with his wealth being estimated at around $US40 billion. His income is close to $US2 billion a year. When his country became independent in 1984, he treated himself to a $US350 million palace and he also owns homes in England, the United States and elsewhere. His extravagance is legendary. His family used to spend so much money at the London jeweller Asprey that they decided to buy it – Prince Jefri Bolkiah of Brunei, the Sultan's brother, led the purchase which cost nearly £250 million. The Sultan, who has been known to pay more than £12,000 for a haircut, has a collection of more than 7,000 high-performance cars including some 600 Rolls Royces, 600 Mercedes (one gold-plated) and more than 300 Ferraris. Brunei is one of the world's most affluent societies and no income tax is payable there. In 2014 Brunei became the first East Asian country to adopt strict Islamic Sharia law which allows punishment such as stoning for adultery and amputation for theft. The country occupies 2,226 square miles in a corner of the island of Borneo and has a population not far short of 450,000.

• Sultan Qaboos bin Said was absolute ruler of Oman since he overthrew his father in a palace coup (supported by Britain) in 1970. The country is a little bigger in area than Britain but has a population of around 4.6 million. The government runs the main broadcasters and censorship is widespread. Freedom House (an independent organisation dedicated to the expansion of freedom and democracy around the world) describes Oman's press law as one of the most restrictive in the Arab world; mobile phone calls, e-mails and chat rooms are all monitored. Libel is a criminal offence and journalists can be fined or imprisoned for criticism of the Sultan or material that leads to "public discord, violates the security of the state, or abuses a person's dignity or rights". Numerous activists have been imprisoned for posting comments online deemed offensive to the Sultan. A graduate of the Sandhurst Military Academy who served for a period in the British Army, he was believed to have a net worth in excess of $US700 million. He died on 10th January 2020 at the age of 79 and was succeeded by his cousin, Haitham bin Tariq Al Said.

• King Abdullah II, who has ruled Jordan since 1999, also trained at the Sandhurst Military Academy and served in the British Army. Technically he is not the head of government but he has considerable political power, including the ability to veto any law and dissolve parliament whenever he wishes. He has an estimated net worth of $US750 million.

• King Bhumibol Adulyadej of Thailand reigned for 67 years from 1950. An accomplished jazz musician, he held a number of constitutional powers, including the ability to veto legislation and pardon criminals. He was cremated a year after his death – and reporters covering that event were banned from having long hair, earrings or moustaches. His son, King Maha Vajiralongkorn, succeeded him. Prior to that he had spent much of his adult life abroad, mostly in Germany, and had become known for a somewhat bizarre and ostentatious lifestyle, on one occasion declaring his favourite pet, a poodle named Foo Foo, an air marshal. He threatened to sue Facebook after footage showed him strolling through a shopping centre in a crop top which revealed his heavily-tattooed body. Since ascending to the throne, the 65-year-old, who had a long military career, has made amendments to the constitution that reinforce his powers. Strict laws make it a crime to criticise, defame or insult members of the royal family, which means open discussion or critical reporting about the royal family is considered illegal. In 2015, a man was jailed for 30 years over six Facebook posts, and numerous others have been convicted for similar offences. The monarchy is believed to be one of the world's wealthiest – with their wealth estimated at over $US30 billion. Meanwhile, the military generals who hold the real power see themselves as royal protectors and have greatly increased prison sentences for dissenters.

• In Morocco, King Mohammed VI voluntarily reduced some of his powers when, in the wake of the Arab Spring uprisings of 2011, he enacted a series of reforms to Morocco's government, a constitutional monarchy. He still appoints the Prime Minister and members of the government but can no longer dissolve the parliament or call for new elections. His wealth is still estimated at just over $US2 billion.

• Liechtenstein, by contrast, actually voted in 2012 to increase the powers of Prince Hans Adam II. Believed to be the richest monarch in Europe – his wealth is estimated at over $US3 billion – he can, among other powers, veto any legislation and dissolve the parliament at will. Technically, many of these official duties have been transferred to his son, Prince Alois, but Hans Adam remains chief of state. Liechtenstein is the second-richest nation after Monaco, with an average per capita income of £85,000 and hundreds of millionaires.

• Prince Albert II has ruled Monaco since 2005 and holds a large political role, despite the fact that Monaco has an elected legislature. The head of the princely house of Grimaldi, he is the son of Prince Rainier III and the American actress Grace Kelly, and another of the billionaire rulers.

• Jigme Khesar Namgyel Wangchuk is the Druk Gyalpo, or Dragon King, of Bhutan. Jigme acceded to the throne in 2008, two years after his father's abdication, giving the 26-year-old time to gain administrative experience. Reforms in the late 1990s reduced the King's powers. The Wangchuck monarchy is just over 100 years old, having unified the small Himalayan country under its rule with help from the British Empire. The current king succeeded Jigme Singye Wangchuck, who coined the term of "Gross National Happiness" in place of GDP and began changing the nation from an absolute monarchy to a constitutional and democratic one.

There are some monarchies (mainly in Europe) which have ceremonial or figurehead monarchs.

Norway's King has a number of important-sounding but entirely ceremonial roles, including appointing the Norwegian cabinet and the Prime Minister, with the approval of the parliament.

Sweden has one of the few monarchies that allows female succession, which means Princess Victoria Ingrid Alice Desiree will become Queen at the end of her father's reign. King Carl XVI Gustaf, the current monarch, is a ceremonial figure and frequently described as "a quietly dignified figure", but a book published in 2010 cataloguing details of his wild youth somewhat dented this image.

The Netherlands' King Willem-Alexander ascended to the throne in 2013 after his mother Beatrix stepped down. The Netherlands has a bicameral parliament, so the monarch doesn't rule directly, but the King still has an important role as President of the Council of State, an advisory body with roots in the 16th century. No law may be submitted to parliament unless it goes to the council first.

King Felipe VI ascended to the Spanish throne in 2014 after his father, King Juan Carlos I, abdicated. He is head of state and commander-in-chief of the Spanish Armed Forces. Rather like Queen Elizabeth with the Commonwealth countries, the king endeavours to promote positive relations with Spain's former colonies.

Moving on from foreign monarchs, let's return to the UK where Queen Elizabeth II is officially titled "Elizabeth the Second, by the Grace of God, of the United Kingdom of Great Britain and Northern Ireland and of Her other Realms and Territories Queen, Head of the Commonwealth, Defender of the Faith". This title was altered in 1953 in order to reflect more clearly the relations of the members of the Commonwealth to one another and their recognition of the Crown as a symbol of their free association. Prior to this, the title had been altered following the independence of India in 1947, to "Elizabeth the Second, by the Grace of God, of Great Britain, Ireland and the British Dominions beyond the Seas, Queen, Defender of the Faith".

The Queen is also deemed to be the "fount of justice" and judicial functions are carried out in her name; and "fount of honour" as all honours in the UK are conferred by the Crown. In addition, "royal assent" is required before an Act passed by parliament becomes law: in theory, assent can either be granted or withheld, but since 1707 assent has never been withheld.

The Queen and members of her family undertake various official, ceremonial, diplomatic and representational duties. As the monarchy is constitutional, the monarch is limited to non-partisan functions such as bestowing honours, "appointing" the Prime Minister and being commander-in-chief of the British Armed Forces. Though the ultimate formal executive authority over the UK government is still by and through the monarch's royal prerogative, these powers may only be used according to laws enacted in parliament and, in practice, within the constraints of convention and precedent. At each State Opening of Parliament, the Queen reads a speech written for her by the government of the day, which she refers to as "my government".

The Queen, who was crowned in 1953, became the world's longest reigning monarch after the death of King Bhumibol Adulyadej of Thailand in 1916. She has given no indication that she has any intention of abdicating, having made clear her commitment to the job for life. Her eldest son, Prince Charles, is a controversial figure and it is possible that the Queen considers it wise to keep him from the throne for as long as possible.

As part of her coronation oath, the Queen was asked by the Archbishop of Canterbury: "Will you to the utmost of your power maintain the Laws of God and the true profession of the Gospel? Will you to the utmost of your power maintain in the United Kingdom the Protestant Reformed Religion established by law? Will you maintain and preserve inviolably the settlement of the Church of England, and the doctrine, worship, discipline, and government thereof, as by law established in England? And will you preserve unto the Bishops and Clergy of England, and to the Churches there committed to their charge, all such rights and privileges, as by law do or shall appertain to them or any of them?" To which she replied: "All this I promise to do."

Thus, the Queen is designated "defender of the faith" (*Fidei Defensor*, in Latin) a title first conferred by Pope Leo X on the appalling Henry VIII in 1521 as a reward for the King's pamphlet *Assertio septem sacramentorum adversus Martinum Lutherum* ("Declaration of the Seven Sacraments Against Martin Luther"). When Henry broke with the papacy, Pope Paul III deprived him of the designation but the title was restored to the King by parliament in 1544 and is still used by his successors on the English throne.

The faith to be defended is clearly spelt out, though no one appears to have much idea of how the Queen actually defends it. The Church of England acknowledges Jesus Christ as its head and the Archbishop of Canterbury as its leader, while the Queen is known as "supreme governor" – quite a title. Prince Charles, however, has let it be known that he would rather be "defender of faiths" – an intriguing notion which, although it might not lead to a constitutional crisis, could have some repercussions. And it will be interesting to see which faiths he wishes to defend.

The prince has also let it be known, or has been reported as saying, at various times that he would not wish to be crowned King Charles because of the association with his beheaded predecessor (he would prefer George); he would not wish to live in Buckingham Palace, though he might acknowledge that the head of state should spend a fair amount of time in the capital city; he would not wish to be silent on some political issues; and so on. When asked why the Prince had staff members working within the civil service, one of his minions said it was preparation for when he (Prince Charles) began to rule the country, ignoring the fact that UK monarchs now reign rather than rule and have precious little say in political matters. The Queen has managed it graciously for more than 60 years, so it can be done.

His younger son, Prince Harry, said in an interview in 2018 that none of the Windsor family wanted to be king but they would do it out of duty. Very magnanimous of him to say so. But, following his marriage and the birth of his son, he has withdrawn from royal duties.

There is also the matter of the lady Prince Charles is married to whom he wishes to see installed as Queen Camilla when he is crowned. A few years back *The Daily Telegraph* published a spread saying that we had all now learned to love Camilla and wanted her to be queen alongside her hubby, while a few days later the *Daily Mail* had a spread telling us that not only had we not come to love Camilla and did not want to see her as queen, but we would prefer not to have Charles as king and we hoped the throne would skip a generation and be given to Charles' eldest son William, a charmingly naïve lad (though the *Daily Mail* didn't call him that). Is there some truth in there somewhere?

There is definitely a clear order of succession so Charles it will be and William will have to wait his turn. There were reports early in 2018 of a bit of friction between the households of the reigning monarch, the heir and the future heir. It's a shame that all is not sweetness and light in the royal households but it is probably to be expected. It will all play out well eventually: Britain is very good at such things.

A report published by the consultancy Brand Finance in November 2017 said that the British monarchy was worth more than £60 billion and boosted the UK economy by £1.7 billion a year (based on 2016 figures), thanks to its effect on tourism, the media and other industries. The chief executive of the consultancy said the monarchy cost very little to run, putting it at the equivalent of 1p per day for each person in the UK.

"It may be a quirky, anomalous, slightly unfair organisation, but economically it is definitely a beneficial one," he said, adding: "The monarchy is Britain's national treasure, both symbolically and economically."

'Property' of, or linked with, the British royal family

The 18,343-hectare private estate known as the Duchy of Lancaster is regarded as the private property of the Queen – who is the Duke of Lancaster – although she cannot sell it. Profits go toward her private and public expenses.

The Duchy includes the Savoy Estate in London, which covers the area between The Strand to the north, Somerset House to the east, the Embankment to the South and the Savoy Hotel to the west; plus rural land in Cheshire, Lancashire, Yorkshire, Staffordshire and the south of England, and the village of Castleton in the Peak District; also included are a dozen or so historic properties including the Savoy Chapel in London, Pickering Castle in Yorkshire and Lancaster Castle in Lancashire.

Sandringham House is owned by the Queen, who inherited it from her father King George VI, along with Balmoral Castle. Both properties were bought by the King from his brother King Edward VIII after his abdication.

The Queen is the legal owner of everything that comes under the Crown Estate, though she does not have controlling rights or access to the revenues.

The Crown Estate is a property portfolio said to be worth over £14 billion – though that is certainly a considerable undervaluation – and certain other assets. It includes the freehold of virtually all of Regent Street in London and half the buildings in St James's. Other assets include some 20 retail parks, shopping centres and leisure destinations, including Oxford's Westgate Centre, Leicester's Fosse Shopping Park, Princesshay in Exeter, Gallagher Shopping Park in Cheltenham and the Crown Gate Centre in Worcester, plus Ascot racecourse. It all "belongs" to the reigning monarch though "surplus" revenue goes to the Treasury. In 2016-17, it paid £328.8 million to the Treasury, which paid 15% (a fixed percentage) of this to the Queen to pay for, among other things, staff costs, property maintenance, travel, utilities and housekeeping. In 2018-19, it returned £345.5 million to the Treasury, a steady increase, and in the last 10 years has returned a total of £2.8 billion.

The Crown Estate is described as a public body which sits outside government (whatever that might mean) and a statutory corporation operating on a commercial basis, the latter under the Crown Estate Act 1961. It is a body established in perpetuity under the Act as a trust estate. "Independent of government and the monarch, The Crown Estate's public function is to: invest in and manage certain property assets belonging to the monarch; and remit its revenue surplus each year to the Exchequer." Curiously, it sold land and property worth £209 million in 2016-17. In that financial year it had "proportionally consolidated revenue" of £462.6 million (mainly from rent and royalties) which included £34 million from its share of joint ventures; its gross surplus was £381.2 million. Staff costs accounted for £33.5 million.

The assets of the Crown Estate in England, Wales and Northern Ireland (in 2017 the management of the assets of the Crown Estate in Scotland were devolved to the Scottish Government), as well as off-shore, are neither the property of the government nor the sovereign's private estate. They are part of the hereditary possessions of the Sovereign "in right of the Crown".

The leadership team at the Crown Estate includes some fascinating titles, such as: director of central London; director of rural and coastal and heads of rural and coastal respectively; director of regional retail; director of energy, minerals and infrastructure; head of energy development; head of Regent Street; head of marine planning; and numerous others.

In its annual report, it states: "We create brilliant places through conscious commercialism. This means we take a long-term view and consider what we do from every perspective."

Buckingham Palace and Windsor Castle are part of the Occupied Royal Palaces Estate and are managed by the Royal Household. The Royal Parks, with the exception of Windsor Great Park which is owned by the Crown Estate, are hereditary possessions of the reigning monarch, and are managed by The Royal Parks section of the Department for Culture, Media and Sport.

The Queen also owns the Royal Collection, one of the world's largest art collections, but nothing can be sold by the reigning monarch. The collection, with an estimated value of about £10 billion, includes the Crown jewels which are stored in the Tower of London.

UK law also states that the reigning monarch owns all the whales, sturgeons and porpoises within three miles of the shore, as well as all unmarked mute swans in open water within the UK. Which is a nice touch.

Despite the fact that many details of the Queen's income are publicly released, her exact wealth is not known. According to the *Sunday Times* Rich List, her personal fortune is estimated to be in the region of £340 million, which includes an investment portfolio valued at well over £100 million.

The Crown Estate dates back to 1760 when George III reached an agreement with the government that surplus revenue from the crown's lands would go to the Treasury. In return, the King no longer had to pay for the cost of civil government and debts accrued by previous monarchs and would receive a fixed annual payment. Every succeeding monarch has renewed the arrangement.

The privy purse, recently valued at about £12.5 million a year, is a private income for the Queen, which is primarily used to pay for expenses incurred by other members of the Royal family. Funds for this come mostly from the Duchy of Lancaster. As with the Crown Estate, the profits from the Duchy of Lancaster go to the Treasury, which then gives funds to the Queen to provide for expenses not covered by the Sovereign Grant.

There is even a government role – the ministerial office of the Chancellor of the Duchy of Lancaster – whose duties include the administration of the estates and rents of the Duchy of Lancaster. The Chancellor is appointed by the Queen on the recommendation of the Prime Minister.

Separately, income from the Duchy of Cornwall funds the private and official expenditure of the Prince of Wales and the Duchess of Cornwall. This is a private estate consisting of 53,408 hectares of land in 23 counties, mostly in the south-west of England, including Devon, Cornwall, Gloucestershire, Somerset and Dorset, as well as Herefordshire and as far afield as Buckinghamshire. It owns a fair-sized portfolio in London, mainly Kennington where its assets include 16 flats, 23 houses and various commercial buildings, including The Oval cricket ground and a number of long leases on other properties. It also owns the Isles of Scilly. In total, the Duchy is nearly one-and-a-half times bigger than the Isle of Wight which is just over 38,000 hectares.

The property includes 23,875 hectares of enclosed farmland, 3,300 hectares of woodland, 160 miles of coastal margins, about 24,000 hectares of mountains, moors and heaths, including 14,150 hectares of peatland and some small areas of urban green space.

The Duchy was created in 1337 by Edward III for his son and heir, Prince Edward. A Charter ruled that each future Duke of Cornwall would be the eldest surviving son of the monarch and the heir to the throne.

The Duchy estate owns about 2% of Cornwall but has "a special relationship" with the county and has certain rights and responsibilities which relate to the county as a whole. It also owns the foreshore (coastline) and fundus (riverbed) around Cornwall and part of south Devon. The property portfolio is estimated to be worth at least £600 million. Running the Duchy is a team of more than 150 people. Included are more than 600 residential lettings and more than 700 agricultural tenancies. The Duchy's annual report for 2017 states: "As well as fulfilling professional obligations as landlord, the estate provides friendly and practical help to support tenants as their needs and priorities change."

A survey of tenants in 2017 asked whether anything could be improved: three-fifths of the comments received were linked to the repairs service or the condition of the property: "Tenants think we could improve our response times for repairs and maintenance issues, and keep them better updated on progress," was the verdict from the Duchy. In other words, pretty much the same problems that have existed since the formation of the Duchy in the 14th century. But now: "There are a number of older houses where tenants want our help to reduce energy bills by improving heating systems and windows."

The question that might be asked is: Why is such a feudal and paternalistic system, based on 14th century principles, still in operation in the 21st century? There must be a better way of funding the lavish lifestyles of heirs to the throne.

Under the 1337 Charter, the Prince is entitled to the annual revenue surplus generated by the estate. The money is used to cover personal and professional expenditure – including staff, charitable work and public duties – for the Prince of Wales and the Duchess of Cornwall, the Duke and Duchess of Cambridge and the Duke and Duchess of Sussex. The income does not cover official travel or property services, which are funded by the Sovereign Grant. Prince Charles "voluntarily" pays income tax at the prevailing rate and has no access to funds from the sale of capital assets. He is the longest-serving Duke of Cornwall and has been actively involved in running the estate.

Without doubt, the vast acreages covered by the Duchy of Lancaster, the Duchy of Cornwall and the Crown Estate could be put to more productive and more profitable use for the good of the nation, but that would require a change far bigger than Brexit. Better left alone!

A regulator in all but name...

While on the subject of the royal family, it's worth taking a look at the role and work of the Privy Council, whose full and rather preposterous title is "Her Majesty's Most Honourable Privy Council". This council is described as "the mechanism through which interdepartmental agreement is reached on those items of government business which, for historical or other reasons, fall to Ministers as Privy Counsellors rather than as Departmental Ministers".

It has a Lord President as its "head" – under the monarch – whose responsibilities include: presiding over Privy Council meetings; considering for approval a number of Statutory Orders concerning healthcare, veterinary, and Scottish Higher Education matters; as a member of the Privy Council Committee for the Affairs of Jersey and Guernsey, reviewing Laws and Orders relating to the Islands, and making recommendations to the monarch concerning their approval; dealing with ministerial correspondence and parliamentary questions relating to Privy Council business, such as the appointment of High Sheriffs.

The Lord President is frequently the leader of the House of Commons and so, in July 2019, the Rt Hon. Jacob Rees-Mogg was appointed to the illustrious office. Past holders of the post have included Peter (now Lord) Mandelson and Nick Clegg (deputy PM in the coalition government of 2010-15).

The Privy Council Office has a clerk and two deputy clerks, one of whom is head of the secretariat, and usually five other officers.

The council has a long history. It was originally comprised of the people appointed by the King or Queen to advise on matters of state. As the "constitution" developed into today's "constitutional monarchy" (constitution in inverted commas because the UK doesn't have much of a written constitution and a lot of it is a matter of convention, supposition, assumption and conjecture), under which the sovereign acts on the advice of ministers, so the Privy Council adapted or evolved. Its normal business is transacted by those of Her Majesty's ministers who are Privy Counsellors – that is all cabinet ministers and a number of junior ministers. Membership of the Privy Council brings with it the right to be called "Right Honourable".

Privy Counsellors swear an oath of allegiance, dating back to the Tudor period, which states: "You do swear by Almighty God to be a true and faithful Servant unto The Queen's (or King's) Majesty as one of Her Majesty's Privy Council. You will not know or understand of any manner of thing to be attempted, done or spoken against Her Majesty's Person, Honour, Crown or Dignity Royal, but you will lett and withstand the same to the uttermost of your power, and either cause it to be revealed to Her Majesty Herself, or to such of Her Privy Council as shall advertise Her Majesty of the same. You will in all things to be moved, treated and debated in Council, faithfully and truly declare your Mind and Opinion, according to your Heart and Conscience; and will keep secret all matters committed and revealed unto you, or that shall be treated of secretly in Council. And if any of the said Treaties or Counsels shall touch any of the Counsellors you will not reveal it unto him but will keep the same until such time as, by the consent of Her Majesty or of the Council, Publication shall be made thereof. You will to your uttermost bear Faith and Allegiance to the Queen's Majesty; and will assist and defend all civil and temporal Jurisdictions, Pre-eminences, and Authorities, granted to Her Majesty and annexed to the Crown by Acts of Parliament, or otherwise, against all Foreign Princes, Persons, Prelates, States, or Potentates. And generally in all things you will do as a faithful and true Servant ought to do to Her Majesty. SO HELP YOU GOD."

The Council's website goes to some length to argue that it is a myth that the Privy Council is a secretive body. "The Oath (or Solemn Affirmation for those who cannot take an Oath) is still administered, and is still binding; but it is only in very special circumstances nowadays that matters will come to a Privy Counsellor on 'Privy Council terms'. These will mostly concern matters of the national interest where it is important for senior members of Opposition parties to have access to government information."

Currently there are nearly 700 – yes, 700 – Privy Counsellors though only four (mainly cabinet ministers) are needed at a meeting. Members include Prince Philip and Prince Charles, the current and former Speakers of the House of Commons, archbishops, senior bishops, senior courtiers, senior backbenchers and senior judges. In practice, its regular meetings are only attended by cabinet or very senior ministers. Appointments are for life and new members are expected to kneel in front of the monarch and kiss her (or his) hand.

Members can be expelled – as Labour MP Elliot Morley was in 2011 after he was sentenced to 16 months in prison following his guilty plea over fiddling £32,000 worth of MPs' expenses. Alternatively they can resign – as did Conservative MP Jonathan Aitken who was imprisoned for perjury in 1999 and resigned rather than be expelled, as well as Liberal Democrat MP Chris Huhne who was imprisoned in 2013 for perverting the course of justice. Departures are, however, fairly rare.

The Privy Council dates from the court of the Norman kings, which met in private – hence the name "privy" – when its members were appointed by the King or Queen to advise on matters of state. It then fulfilled the role that the cabinet performs today and, in effect, the cabinet is still a committee of the Privy Council.

In layman's terms, as explained on the BBC's website, "the PC's role is to advise the monarch of the day in carrying out his or her duties, such as the exercise of prerogative powers and other functions assigned to the monarch by Acts of Parliament. Much of its business is rather routine and is concerned with obtaining the monarch's formal approval to orders which have already been discussed and approved by ministers or for the arranging for the issuing of royal proclamations".

It has formally to approve changes to the governance of institutions, charities and companies which are incorporated by Royal Charter, as well as universities and professional regulatory bodies. It also has to rubber-stamp ministerial changes, appointments to government bodies and the appointment of High Sheriffs in England and Wales; and issue "commencement orders" which state when Acts or sections of Acts of Parliament come into effect.

It is also the court of final appeal for the UK's overseas territories and Crown Dependencies, and for those Commonwealth countries that have retained the appeal to Her Majesty in Council, including Jamaica, Barbados, Antigua and Barbuda, Belize and Tuvalu.

According to the government's website, decisions of the Privy Council are recorded and expressed through "Orders" which have the force of law. Most

"Orders" are government decisions, drawn up by ministers and civil servants, which are then "approved by the Queen in Her Privy Council as a matter of course". There are two main types of "Orders". Orders *in* Council are those that have been approved personally by the Queen at a meeting of the Privy Council; while Orders *of* Council do not require the personal approval of the Queen and can be made by the "Lords of the Privy Council" – that is, by government ministers.

So these Orders ("laws") can be introduced without the need to consult parliament. However, the Privy Council is rarely involved in matters which might be considered controversial.

To date, for instance, more than 980 Royal Charters have been granted and about 750 remain in existence. The earliest was to the town of Tain in 1066, making it the oldest Royal Burgh in Scotland, followed by the University of Cambridge in 1231. New grants of Royal Charters are, says the Privy Council, nowadays "reserved for eminent professional bodies or charities which have a solid record of achievement and are financially sound. In the case of professional bodies they should represent a field of activity which is unique and not covered by other professional bodies.

"Once incorporated by Royal Charter, a body surrenders significant aspects of the control of its internal affairs to the Privy Council. Amendments to Charters can be made only with the agreement of The Queen in Council, and amendments to the body's by-laws require the approval of the Council (though not normally of the monarch). This effectively means a significant degree of government regulation of the affairs of the body, and the Privy Council will therefore wish to be satisfied that such regulation accords with public policy."

Since the MCC (Marylebone Cricket Club) received a Charter in 2012, others have been granted (to the end of 2017) to: The Marine Biological Association of the United Kingdom; Worshipful Company of Furniture Makers; The Worshipful Livery Company of Wales; Worshipful Company of Hackney Carriage Drivers; The Worshipful Company of Chartered Surveyors; The Worshipful Company of World Traders; Chartered Association of Building Engineers; The Chartered Institute of Horticulture; The Chartered Society of Forensic Sciences; The Recognition Panel; The Worshipful Company of Firefighters; Honourable Company of Air Pilots; The Chartered Institute for Archaeologists; Chartered Institute of Ergonomics and Human Factors; The Worshipful Company of Fuellers; Chartered Trading Standards Institute; Chartered Institute of Credit Management; The Chartered Association of Business Schools; The Worshipful Company of Insurers; The

Chartered Institution for Further Education; Learned Society of Wales; The Institute of Practitioners in Advertising; The Chartered Institute of Trade Mark Attorneys; Association for Project Management; National Citizen Service Trust; Worshipful Company of Educators; and Police Roll of Honour Trust.

That is quite a lot – and it seems almost any organisation or body can get one. But there is no mention in the list of the Royal Charter on Self-Regulation of the Press issued in 2014. As we saw in the section on regulation of the press, this was highly unusual in that it was a Charter imposed rather than sought by a body and is proving to be remarkably ineffective – and it didn't meet the Privy Council's basic requirements for a Royal Charter. While it might have been sparked by good intentions, it appears to have been much more of an attempt by the government of the day to circumvent parliament and impose on the press a scheme of regulation which the majority resoundingly rejected.

Intriguingly, this Charter can only be amended by a two-thirds majority of each of the House of Commons, the House of Lords and the Scottish Parliament, and with the unanimous agreement of the Press Recognition Panel's (PRP) Board members. It may, therefore, be with us, if in name only, for quite a long time.

Politics – 2

Britain's greatest Prime Minister?

Margaret Hilda Thatcher was Prime Minister of the UK from May 1979 until November 1990 and is regarded by many as one of the nation's greatest leaders, although to a goodly number of others she is little more than "that dreadful woman".

She made a promising start. Standing outside 10 Downing Street after being declared the winner of the 1979 general election, she said: "I would just like to remember some words of St Francis of Assisi which I think are really just particularly apt at the moment. 'Where there is discord, may we bring harmony. Where there is error, may we bring truth. Where there is doubt, may we bring faith. And where there is despair, may we bring hope.'"

There were one or two things that weren't quite right about this. First, there is no evidence to suggest that St Francis, who lived around the turn of the 13th century, ever said or wrote the words (they appear to have first appeared in 1912); and second, it became clear within a few weeks that Mrs T had no intention of trying to bring harmony, truth, faith or hope – at least not to the masses.

It's true that she wanted to bring order into the economy, to balance the books, to develop a free market economy, cast off what she saw as the shackles imposed by trade unions, and so on. But anyone who opposed her views was immediately classified as "not one of us" and ignored.

There were severe challenges facing the country at the time. The economy was not in good shape and unemployment was high, so much so that the Conservatives campaigned against the previous Labour government under the slogan, "Labour isn't working". Unemployment at the time was between five and six per cent of the working population; it went on to peak at 11.9% (3 million people) in 1984 – a little short of the midway point of Mrs T's premiership – and, apart from a spell in the first decade of this century, it has been quite a bit above 6% until the last few years.

Sir Geoffrey Howe was appointed Chancellor of the Exchequer in Mrs Thatcher's first cabinet – and his first budget caused quite a stir. He stated: "Our strategy to check Britain's long-term economic decline, which has gathered pace in the last five years, is based on four principles. We need to strengthen incentives, by allowing people to keep more of what they earn, so that hard work, talent and ability are properly rewarded. We need to enlarge freedom of choice for the individual by reducing the role of the State. We need to reduce the burden of financing the public sector, so as to leave room for commerce and industry to prosper. We need to ensure, so far as possible, that those who take part in collective bargaining understand the consequences of their actions – for that is the way to promote a proper sense of responsibility." Ominous words for many.

He went on to announce his intention to switch some of the tax burden from taxes on earnings to taxes on spending. "This is the only way that we can restore incentives and make it more worthwhile to work and, at the same time, increase the freedom of choice of the individual." So VAT was raised from 8% to 15%.

He said: "There are many cogent arguments at this stage in favour of value added tax. First, large areas of consumer spending, in fact about half the total, are not chargeable to VAT. Food, children's clothes, heating and light, public transport, house prices and rents are all zero rated. Second, poorer households tend to spend proportionately more of their income on such zero-rated goods. This means that, unlike most indirect taxes, VAT is not regressive."

Now that was a comment of mind-boggling stupidity – but it was in line with a strand of Conservative thinking that still prevails. To Conservatives, labour is simply a cost of production and the more that companies can reduce their costs, the greater their profit is likely to be. Standard economic theory. Poor people can get much of what they need tax-free but if they want to raise their living standards they'll have to pay heavily for it. VAT is a savagely regressive tax and the consequences of Sir Geoffrey's comments soon became clear.

He went on to state: "I fully realise that this increase in value added tax will result in a rise in prices – in fact, a rise of about 3½% in the retail price index. This is, of course, a once-for-all effect. But there never will be a time when it is easy to effect the switch from direct to indirect taxes, and the present moment is clearly no exception. That much-needed reform has been postponed too long already."

To "compensate" for the rise in VAT, he reduced the bottom rate of income tax from 33% to 30%.

We are nowadays used to hearing the term "unintended consequences" when actions have consequences that the perpetrator, in this case the government, did not intend. But this should not be confused with "unforeseen consequences". Warnings of outcomes different from those the government wanted or hoped for were simply ignored – as they still are. This happened

141

time and again with the economic policies of the era, not least with the introduction of the Community Charge (or poll tax) in Scotland in 1989 and in England and Wales in 1990. But we shall come back to that.

The policy of allowing people to keep more of their own money when they got paid while making anything other than basic requirements considerably more expensive backfired. We witnessed a near doubling in the level of unemployment over the next several years. Mrs Thatcher had declared that companies would prosper under her new regime and as unemployment rose sharply she simply declared that companies would emerge "leaner and fitter" from the carnage. Unfortunately, many did not emerge at all.

The financial cost to the government of this huge increase in unemployment – the loss of both income tax and corporation tax revenue, reduced personal spending capabilities which saw a drop in the amount of VAT collected, the social security and dole payments, etc. – severely limited her ambitions, and this was at a time when the country should have been prospering with peak revenues from North Sea oil.

At the time, Sir Geoffrey received high praise from the captains of the major industries and even many economists for this budget but it wreaked considerable havoc upon the nation.

Towards the end of his budget speech, he said: "I have stressed the urgent need for new policies to reverse the decline of the British economy. These policies start with our conviction that it is people and not governments who create prosperity. This Budget seeks to reduce the role of government. Government will spend less, government will borrow less. This will lay the foundations for controlling inflation."

Ah, if only things were that easy.

Not long after Mrs Thatcher's departure from office, in May 1991 the Chancellor, Norman Lamont, said: "Rising unemployment and the recession have been the price that we have had to pay to get inflation down. That price is well worth paying." He may well have thought so. But rising unemployment and recession had been a long way from Sir Geoffrey's mind when he presented his first budget 11 years earlier.

Eventually, however, income tax rates did come down – while the rate of VAT went even higher, to the punishing level of 20% in 2012 (and still at that rate more than seven years later); however, inflation, which fluctuated wildly for many years, was largely under control in the first period of this century. So we had a lot of pain for small gain.

Mrs Thatcher's plans for the economy were thrown into disarray by the events which followed that first budget, but she was determined to stay the

142

course. "This lady's not for turning," became one of her catchphrases; another, relating specifically to economic policy, was: "There is no alternative!" (abbreviated to TINA). There were, as there always are in economic matters, plenty of alternatives – but Mrs T's stubbornness and pride allowed no giving in or change of course. Great leaders will make changes when they are clearly called for but Mrs Thatcher, although she had a number of sterling qualities, could not count flexibility among them.

With her popularity waning, Mrs T needed something to give her a boost and enable her to reassert her authority – and the chance came when Argentina invaded the British Territory of the Falkland Islands in the south Atlantic on 2nd April 1982. Her response produced the high point of her term in office – as well as the lowest, although she might not have seen it that way.

The two main islands in the Falklands occupy about the same area as Wales – in 1982 they had a population of 1,820 people and 400,000 sheep. Against some spirited opposition, Mrs Thatcher took the bold decision to send a task force to recapture the territory. This arrived on 1st May and quickly retook South Georgia, moving on to the slower process of reclaiming the main islands, which took several weeks before the Argentinians surrendered – a genuine military triumph. The British lost 250 men and captured 12,278 prisoners; five civilians died. The Argentines had 746 killed, nearly half of whom were on a ship sunk by two British torpedoes fired by a British "hunter-killer" submarine.

The UK had established a 200-mile naval exclusion zone around the area to keep ships out and the Argentinian high command certainly took notice of this. One of its vessels, an ageing cruiser, *General Belgrano*, was outside this zone when spotted by a British submarine. Mrs Thatcher was consulted and gave the order for it to be sunk – despite it not being within the zone. There is some dispute about whether it was sailing away from or closer to the zone, but no dispute that it had not crossed into it. This decision somehow escaped an investigation by an international war crimes tribunal but it was certainly one of the low points in British military history – and of Mrs Thatcher's time in office.

The war went a long way to restoring Mrs Thatcher's popularity and she comfortably won the general election the following year: although the Tories received 700,000 fewer votes than in 1979, they won considerably more seats and their parliamentary majority increased from 43 to 144. With unemployment rising so rapidly in her first term and the need to keep inflation under control, Mrs T looked for alternative ways to put some spending money into the government's coffers – and selling off state assets and businesses seemed a logical choice to her. She, along with many in her party, believed that privatisation would make the large utilities more efficient and productive.

There was no doubt that some of the big nationalised industries, particularly British Gas and British Telecom, were little short of hopeless, offering customer service that ranged from poor to dreadful, resisting innovation and generally being arrogant and unhelpful. British Airways wasn't in the same class, but it was an easy target for privatisation. Some of the later privatisations, particularly water and rail, were daft and almost nothing good has come out of them. In her second term as Prime Minister, 22 privatisations were completed or well under way.

The privatisation programme made quite a lot of leaders of the industries very wealthy and banks and other financial institutions also did extremely well. The programme opened the way for one of the most corrupt periods in UK politics and business life and quite a number of Mrs T's favoured businessmen ended up in prison. Every upside has a down!

There were other notable achievements: the industrial power of the trade union movement was drastically reduced and days lost through strike action fell sharply; the coal miners' union was faced down and although ministers lied about the effects on the industry, Mrs T gained a notable victory; share ownership rose sharply, particularly as a result of the privatisations; home ownership also rose after permission was granted to allow the sale of council houses; and we had "the big bang" which transformed the stock market.

On the downside, Mrs Thatcher used the police on a number of occasions to sort out, often with considerable force, industrial disputes and this politicising of the police force was deplorable. When it came to taxation, her government gave the Inland Revenue, now HMRC, the right to treat all taxpayers, whether corporate or private, as guilty unless they could prove their innocence, and to instigate inquiries into any of them without any suspicion of wrongdoing and without regard to the costs incurred by taxpayers in dealing with the in-depth investigations. Guilt could be presumed – though only until a case reached the courts. HMRC went on to crack down mercilessly on the lower paid while making generous deals with international corporations.

Mrs Thatcher called a general election in June 1987, winning a third term with a comfortable but reduced majority of 102 seats. Unemployment had fallen below the 3 million mark and inflation was, at 4%, as low as it had been for a good many years.

After the 1983 general election, Nigel Lawson replaced Sir Geoffrey Howe as Chancellor and promised an end to "boom and bust" in the economy. There was strong growth from 1985 to 1988 but by 1990 inflation had increased to

9.5% and the economy was in a classic "boom and bust" cycle. And so, just 10 years after Mrs T's first chancellor plunged the economy into recession, her second one led the country into an even deeper one.

Had Mrs Thatcher stepped down as Prime Minister after seven years (*see earlier comments re "best before" dates for leaders*) she would have been remembered as a decisive leader who made some bold, though not altogether popular, decisions, leaving the country in pretty good shape for the years ahead. But, as with most leaders, the elixir of power made her stay on.

Her last years in office were marked by the fall towards recession, some rather dodgy privatisations (having started, she couldn't resist the urge to continue) and the introduction of the poll tax (though her government preferred the title Community Charge).

Mrs Thatcher was urged to press ahead with the tax by one of her policy advisers in 10 Downing Street, Oliver Letwin, who went on to become a cabinet minister and was Chancellor of the Duchy of Lancaster from 2014 to 2016. Papers published in December 2014 reveal that the Prime Minister had been deluged with warnings about the catastrophic political consequences of the tax, including one from her Chancellor of the Exchequer, Nigel Lawson, but went ahead anyway.

Pushed through parliament after the 1987 general election, it is among the daftest pieces of legislation enacted in the last 60 years and had entirely predictable results. A savagely regressive tax, it had no merit whatsoever; there was large-scale rebellion, culminating in a huge demonstration-cum-riot of about 100,000 people in central London, and the new Prime Minister, John Major, scrapped it barely a year later, when the then environment secretary, Michael Heseltine (who had been regarded as a "wet" by Mrs Thatcher for his views on her economic policies and was too far to the left for her liking) announced a property tax to replace it.

At the time, Heseltine said, "The new tax should reflect people's ability to pay, be easy to collect and be seen to be fair," which should be the basis of all taxation but for some reason wasn't favoured by Mrs Thatcher.

After a speech in which she declared she wanted "to go on and on and on", the Conservatives realised Mrs T had become more of a liability than an asset and she left Downing Street in tears after being ousted. It was an ignominious end which could so easily have been avoided had the good lady been aware of the time limits on good leadership.

After leaving office, in 1992 – the same year in which she received a life peerage and became Baroness Thatcher – she signed on as an international consultant to the Philip Morris tobacco company at a pay rate of $US500,000 annually, with half to be paid directly to her and half to her Foundation. Reports said the company would seek her advice on controversial issues including the penetration of tobacco markets in Eastern Europe and the Third World, and also her help in resisting attempts to ban tobacco advertising in the European Community and to fight cigarette taxes and state-run tobacco monopolies. This might well explain why tougher action was not taken against sales of tobacco while she was in power, when she, along with members of her cabinet[1] and even senior civil servants, received considerable hospitality from tobacco firms.

It was also reported that Philip Morris paid about $US1,000,000 for a 70th birthday party for Mrs Thatcher in October 1995 in Washington DC, which was attended by about 800 guests.

So: one of the greatest ever British Prime Ministers? Possibly. Her main competitor for the fantasy title is Winston Churchill, another politician who proved to be a great wartime leader but who was also one of the most bigoted and racially prejudiced of the nation's premiers.

Of recent contenders, only Tony Blair (1997-2007), who also won three elections, comes anywhere close, but his reputation was well on the downhill slide in his second term and his "best before" date came some way short of the 6.5 year mark. John Major (1990-1997) displayed few leadership skills; Gordon Brown[2] (2007-2010) was temperamentally unsuited to the job; as mentioned earlier, David Cameron (2010-2016) proved a lightweight – in Barack Obama's words; and of the hapless Theresa May, the less said the better.

How come a country such as the UK produces so few capable leaders while the ones it does produce remain in power for too long?

How different things might have been if Margaret Thatcher had stood down in 1985. We might have had a totally different set of PMs since then. But we can only dream.

---

1. Kenneth Clarke, who held several ministerial posts under Mrs Thatcher and several more, including Chancellor of the Exchequer (1993-1997), under John Major and also served in David Cameron's cabinet, was another who forged close links with the tobacco industry and was for a time paid £170,000 as deputy chairman of BAT, then the second largest tobacco multinational in the world with 15% of the world cigarette market. He was also known as BAT Director for Corporate Social Responsibility, which internal BAT memos described as providing "air cover" and "publicly endorsed amnesty" for the company. Described as "an ardent pro-tobacco advocate", he was appointed the first Secretary of State for Health when the department was created out

of the former Department of Health and Social Security in 1988. This might go some way to explaining why the UK was practically the last country in the developed world to accept that smoking was a major cause of lung cancer. The Department of Health kept stating for many years that no link had been proven – until its protestations became just too ridiculous. Among his work for BAT: in 1999 he attended a meeting in Geneva at which BAT discussed with its competitors how they might resist advertising bans proposed in a draft international treaty, and in 2001 he went to Vietnam to help smooth the way for BAT's joint ventures in that country.

2. Gordon Brown was Chancellor of the Exchequer for all of Tony Blair's time as PM (1997-2007) and in the early years made a pretty good fist of the job. "Prudence" was his watchword and he even reportedly repaid some of the national debt. Gradually, however, he loosened the reins and got into social engineering with the noble aim of helping the poorer people in society. Unfortunately, it proved ruinously expensive, "prudence" was cast off, and the economy headed on a downward spiral towards another recession. His scheme was not only a difficult one for claimants to fathom but was also wide open to fraudulent claims. As one senior banker commented a short time before everything went pear-shaped in 2007, "Gordon Brown is certainly not afraid to make things complicated."

Politics – 3

Overseas aid and health:
why not tackle the pressing problems?

The 2017 World Malaria Report from the World Health Organisation (WHO) showed that after "an unprecedented period of success in global malaria control", progress had stalled. In 2016 (the latest accurate figures available as this was written) there were an estimated 216 million cases of malaria, an increase of about 5 million cases over 2015. Deaths reached 445,000, a similar number to the previous year. The report drew on data from 91 countries and areas with ongoing malaria transmission.

The WHO reported that, of 56.9 million deaths worldwide in 2016, more than half (54%) were due to the top 10 causes. Ischaemic heart disease and stroke are the world's biggest killers, accounting for a combined 15.2 million deaths in 2016. These diseases have remained the leading causes of death globally in the last 15 years.

Chronic obstructive pulmonary disease claimed 3 million lives in 2016, while lung cancer (along with tracheal and bronchial cancers) caused 1.7 million deaths. Diabetes killed 1.6 million people, up from less than 1 million in 2000. Deaths due to dementias more than doubled between 2000 and 2016, making it the fifth leading cause of global deaths in 2016, compared to 14th in 2000.

Lower respiratory infections remained the most deadly communicable disease, causing 3 million deaths worldwide in 2016. The death rate from diarrhoeal diseases decreased by almost a million between 2000 and 2016, but still caused 1.4 million deaths in 2016. Similarly, the number of tuberculosis deaths decreased during the same period, but is still among the top 10 causes with a death toll of 1.3 million. HIV/AIDS is no longer among the world's top 10 causes of death, having killed about a million people in 2016 compared to 1.5 million in 2000.

More than half of all deaths in low-income countries in 2016 were caused by the so-called "Group I" conditions, which include communicable diseases, maternal causes, conditions arising during pregnancy and childbirth, and nutritional deficiencies. By contrast, less than 7% of deaths in high-income countries were due to such causes. Lower respiratory infections were among the leading causes of death across all income groups.

Rabies is a vaccine-preventable viral disease which occurs in more than 150 countries and territories and causes tens of thousands of deaths every year, mainly in Asia and Africa. Dogs are the main source of human rabies deaths, contributing up to 99% of all rabies transmissions to humans, but rabies elimination is feasible, says the WHO, through vaccination of dogs and prevention of dog bites. Two-fifths of people bitten by suspect rabid animals are children under 15 years of age.

Non-communicable diseases (NCDs) caused 71% of deaths globally, ranging from 37% in low-income countries to 88% in high-income countries. All but one of the 10 leading causes of death in high-income countries were NCDs.

But the WHO noted that many low- and middle-income countries do not have adequate recording systems so it has to estimate numbers of deaths from specific causes from incomplete data.

All these figures reveal that while a great deal of progress has been made, there is a very long way to go in eliminating diseases – particularly malaria, tuberculosis and rabies – that are relatively easy to prevent and a huge gap between progress in the rich nations and those at the lower end of the scale.

There are also big differences in the health of men and women. The WHO reports that, worldwide, women live an average four years longer than men with women's life expectancy at birth more than 80 years in 46 countries but only 58 years in much of Africa. Almost all (99%) of the 287,000 (approximately) maternal deaths every year occur in developing countries. Girls are also far more likely than boys to suffer sexual abuse. Tuberculosis is often linked to HIV infection and is among the five leading causes of death in low-income countries among women of reproductive age and among adult women aged between 20 and 59.

"Air" and "water" are both serious problems.

In 2016, 91% of the world's population did not breathe clean air, and more than half of urban populations were exposed to outdoor air pollution levels at least 2.5 times above the safety standard set by WHO. It has been estimated that in 2016 outdoor air pollution in both cities and rural areas caused 4.2 million deaths worldwide. Taken together, indoor and outdoor air pollution caused an estimated 7 million deaths – one in eight deaths – globally that year.

Also according to the WHO, 844 million people lack even a basic drinking-water service, including 159 million people who are dependent on surface water, and at least 2 billion people use a drinking water source contaminated

149

with faeces. Contaminated drinking water is estimated to cause 502,000 diarrhoeal deaths each year. In low- and middle-income countries, 38% of healthcare facilities lack an improved water source, 19% do not have improved sanitation, and 35% lack water and soap for handwashing.

According to a joint report from the WHO and UNICEF in 2017, "The data we have now are more than enough to show the tasks at hand: to eliminate open defaecation for the nearly 900 million people who continue to lack even the most rudimentary sanitation; to bring basic water, sanitation and hygiene within the reach of the most disadvantaged; and to support progress for those who already have basic services, but still don't have truly safe drinking water or adequate sanitation."

It also said: "Of the 159 million people still collecting drinking water directly from surface water sources, 58% live in sub-Saharan Africa."

In August 2017, *National Geographic* published an interview with actor Matt Damon, a co-founder of Water.org, an organisation that promotes access to safe water and sanitation and is currently active in Ethiopia, Ghana, Kenya, Tanzania, Uganda, Bangladesh, Cambodia, India, Indonesia, Philippines, Brazil, Honduras and Peru. He stated that 2.4 billion people lack adequate access to sanitation and more people have a cell phone than a toilet. An article elsewhere in the issue said that nearly a billion people, more than half of them in India, defaecate outdoors every day. The result, said the article: millions of deaths and disease-stunted lives. "The problem isn't just a lack of toilets – it's a lack of toilets that people want to use."

Alarming statistics in the article included this: "Diseases caused by poor sanitation and unsafe water kill more children, some 1.4 million per year, than measles, malaria and AIDS combined."

Other charities such as Oxfam and Save the Children are working in countries such as Yemen and South Sudan to improve both water quality and sanitation, but wars and famine coupled with natural disasters are making many of the problems even worse.

The UK government is required, by its own law, to spend 0.7% of gross national income on overseas development assistance – foreign aid. In 2015, according to the Department for International Development, that translated to a total spend of £12.1 billion, in 2016 to £13.4 billion and was expected to keep steadily rising – if the economy grew. According to forecasts by the Office for Budget Responsibility, the UK could be spending about £14.5 billion in 2021.

In 2015, 37% of this aid was delivered via international organisations and 63% was spent as bilateral aid sent directly to the countries concerned. The top five country recipients of UK aid in 2017 were Pakistan, Syria, Ethiopia,

Nigeria and Afghanistan, followed by Tanzania, Jordan, South Sudan, Sierra Leone and Somalia. In terms of continents, Africa got 51% and Asia 42%.

"Overseas aid" has been controversial for a long time and, for all the vast expenditure, there has often been rather too little to show for it. Both Conservative and Labour governments in the 1980s and 90s were embarrassed when it emerged that financial aid was being given to Malaysia and Turkey in exchange for arms deals with UK companies. The *Guardian* newspaper said the Labour government's involvement in the Ilisu dam in Turkey "may be the biggest corruption scandal in western Europe". Earlier, the Conservatives, according to the *Guardian*, misdirected some £200 million to finance a white elephant project (the Pergau dam) in Malaysia, through an obscure funding mechanism called the Aid and Trade Provision. The governments at the time were determined to secure contracts for both arms manufacturers and a major construction company.

And the UK is still giving "aid" to countries which really don't need it, including China which received £27.4 million in 2017. Government officials said this money went towards schemes to combat climate change and help boost economic growth. But it flew in the face of government assurances that the programme had ended after China – along with 15 other nations – was judged ineligible for British aid. Indeed, ministers had concluded in 2010 that it was no longer justifiable to channel public funds to an economic superpower.

About 15% of the overseas aid budget is spent on "humanitarian aid" or crisis relief; with the rest supposedly spent on "strategic or long-term goals". "Health" was allocated 12% and "education" 11%. More than a third of the money goes via multilateral organisations, like the United Nations; the bulk of the rest going to programmes in specific countries as bilateral aid.

The severely troubled and muddled Department for International Development (DfID) is responsible for most of the UK's aid spending, disposing of three-quarters of the total spend; while the rest is spent by other government departments and organisations.

Spending counts as overseas development assistance if: (1) it goes towards a specific list of low- and middle-income countries, or institutions like the World Bank; (2) it is spent by the government or government agencies; (3) its main aim is to promote economic development and welfare; (4) it is a grant, or a loan that gives the borrower a much better deal than a loan at market rate.

A report by the Independent Commission for Aid Impact (ICAI) in 2014 found that taxpayers' money spent abroad was "actively encouraging corrupt practices". This body scrutinises UK aid spending. It says: "We operate independently of government and report to parliament through the House of Commons International Development Committee or their ICAI Sub-Committee. We work to ensure UK aid is spent effectively for those who need it most, and delivers value for UK taxpayers."

The ICAI reports to the International Development Committee (IDC), a select committee of the House of Commons, whose job is to examine the expenditure, administration and policy of the Department for International Development and its associated public bodies. In 2018, the IDC said that aid delivered under a multi-million-pound cross-government "prosperity fund" was insufficiently focused on poverty reduction and lacked transparency.

The prosperity fund's emphasis on promoting British trade was a step towards tied aid, the MPs said, noting that tied aid was a concept discredited after Britain's previous "aid for arms" scandals.

Projects supported by the prosperity fund – which is administered by the Foreign Office and which paid out £46 million in 2017 – included development of the Chinese film industry, improving the Chinese museum infrastructure and improving the credit bond rating system in China. These are somewhat strange uses for UK taxpayers' money.

In April 2016, the public accounts committee of the House of Commons reported that the government had been giving money from its foreign aid budget to third parties without a full understanding of how those funds would be spent in humanitarian crises. This followed revelations that £6 million had been given to a think-tank in the USA and other money had been paid to Palestinians suspected of terrorism.

Later that year *The Times* reported that "billions of pounds in overseas aid money had been dumped into obscure World Bank trust funds in an apparent attempt to meet the country's controversial annual target". At least £9 billion had gone into 219 different trusts and the World Bank had charged the UK more than £240 million in administrative fees over the period.

The UK has not been alone in making a hash of spending its overseas aid budget. In 2016, a report by the European parliament said that development aid worth £11.5 billion a year was being "thrown down the toilet" because of poor management and corruption in Arab and African countries. It reported that half the EU's annual aid budget of £23 billion missed its target, with every second euro spent by the EU not achieving what it pays for.

The question which appears not to be asked is: with all the problems associated with health, water quality and sanitation, why is the bulk of British overseas aid not used to help reduce these "humanitarian" problems and to seek to improve the lives of the millions upon millions of people living in sub-standard conditions without proper access to even the most basic requirements?

That would make much more sense than helping the Chinese film industry. And oversee it properly so that the money doesn't end up in the hands of tyrants or in Swiss or other bank accounts. Get a grip!

And ensure, in the words of the ICAI, that UK aid – our money – is spent effectively for those who need it most.

Musings

What a wacky world ...

It's difficult not to enjoy – or be puzzled or amazed by – some of the dafter things that happen. The following is but a tiny selection, some personal, of weird, wonderful and sometimes appalling occurrences and comments noted down the years that have provoked reactions ranging from laughter to incredulity or shock. It seemed a good way to finish…

'Absolute consideration' given to mind-boggling decision

It was revealed in August 2017 that Tower Hamlets (an East London borough) council had placed a "white Christian girl" not just once, but twice, with Muslim families whose knowledge of English was extremely limited. A spokesman for the council said (perhaps inevitably), "We are unable to comment on individual cases…," adding: "Tower Hamlets council fostering service provides a loving and stable home for hundreds of children every year, and in every case we give absolute consideration to our children's background and to their cultural identity." How could you argue with that!

Not a very high opinion of civil servants

In 2011, David Cameron, Prime Minister of the UK from May 2010 until July 2016, said (or let slip, as it was reported) that he regarded civil servants as "the enemies of enterprise". This reflected the view of quite a number of government ministers including Liam Fox who commissioned a review of the management at the Ministry of Defence because "it has been the worst run of all departments in recent years", quite a claim when you consider how badly other departments, particularly the Home Office, have been run.

Protocols. What protocols? Who cares?

"Brexit is a very complex problem." That is what the American President, Donald Trump, said the Queen had told him during their afternoon tea break at Windsor Castle in July 2018. Hardly a startling revelation but the leader of the free world (so-called) was accused of breaching protocol by revealing what Her Majesty had said. It's apparently not the done thing. Mr Trump was also accused by some of breaching protocol by not bowing to the monarch, but US protocols insist that the POTUS need not bow to anyone. In addition, *The Times* reported another apparent breach of protocol, stating that Mr Trump had been 12 minutes late for his meeting with the Queen; a few days later the paper published, in small print, a "correction", stating that the president had actually arrived on time.

Keep out of the Chinese Presidents' way

In July 2015 the Home Office refused to grant a visa to the well-known Chinese artist and dissident, Ai Weiwei, on the grounds that he had failed to declare a criminal conviction – even though he had never been convicted of any crime. This ludicrous but not untypical decision was actually taken to prevent him from being in the UK at the same time as the Chinese President. The decision was described as shameful by all sorts of people and groups but this department knows no shame. Al Weiwei, who designed the main stadium for the Beijing Olympics in 2008, was eventually granted a restricted 20-day visa to allow him to open an exhibition of his work at the Royal Academy of Arts in London but to ensure he was gone before the president's arrival. During the President's visit an 81-year-old "Free Tibet" protester was threatened with arrest after failing to move when police officers asked her to.

• In a similar vein, when the Chinese President Hu Jintao visited the UK in November 2005, the police confiscated posters and placards being held by peaceful protesters on the route he was taking through London. No one would take responsibility for requesting this illegal action though it subsequently emerged that 10 Downing Street had "let it be known" they would prefer not to have Mr Hu see anything that might disturb him and the Home Office had "let it be known" that it would like some action to be taken. It became clear that the Metropolitan Police acted on these vague "let it be knowns". Apparently that was how the system worked during Mr Blair's premiership. Prince Charles declined to attend the State banquet on both occasions because he disapproved of Beijing's treatment of the Dalai Lama. China disapproves of anyone meeting with this rather charming gentleman because they replaced him with someone else after annexing Tibet, making the outrageous claim that the country had always really been a part of China. The Chinese government knew that no other country would come to Tibet's aid.

Some reluctance to fund the Conservative Party

A donor to both the Brexit campaign and the Conservative Party was reported to have asked, "Why do we fund this shitshow?" during a gathering of party faithful at the Hurlingham Club in London in July 2018. Several donors were present at the event: they funded both the bash and the party, they said. But they appeared a little underwhelmed by something or other.

An error to be looked into...

In August 2017 the Home Office sent letters to 100 EU citizens telling them they faced detention and removal from the UK. But it was all a mistake. The letters, from an office in Sheffield, had been sent, said the Home Office, "in error". A Home Office spokesman said it was looking into how the error occurred. Good on them.

A tax system not fit for purpose

In January 2014 a gathering of leading chief executives of UK businesses described Britain's tax system as "not fit for purpose" and the results of the annual survey by PricewaterhouseCoopers (PwC), published at the same time, revealed that 73% of CEOs believed the tax system was not fit for the 21st century while 72% said efforts to reform it would be in vain. Interestingly, 66% of them believed that companies with international divisions should be required to publish the revenues, profits and taxes paid for each country in which they operated.

Kind-hearted organisations
agree to payment by instalments

In 2015 a pensioner in Derbyshire, living on little more than the state pension, was startled to receive a letter from HMRC stating that he owed tax of £7.4 billion but he could pay in five monthly instalments of just £950 million. When he got through to the tax department on the phone, he was told there might have been an error. He was then directed to contact a different department and said afterwards that it seemed easier to get an audience with the Pope than speak to the relevant person at HMRC. A spokesman for HMRC was later quoted as saying, "We are very sorry about the error."

The UK doesn't have a monopoly on such stupidity. In 2012, a self-employed child-minder in France received a telephone bill for €11.7 million billion – more than 5,000 times the country's gross national product. The company initially said, courteously, that she could pay the amount in instalments but later did admit to making an error. The bill should have been €117.21.

Probate fees increase gets
great response from Ministry

In February 2017 the Ministry of Justice announced a substantial rise in probate fees, from £215 to up to £20,000; although no fee would be payable on estates worth up to £50,000, the threshold having been raised from the existing one of £5,000. The MoJ said its "fairer banded system" would mean that 92% of estates would pay no more than £1,000, barely five times more than before, though some would pay 129 times more. A ministry spokesman said (and you can almost sense his nose extending as he spoke): "Fees are necessary to maintain an accessible, world-leading justice system, which puts the needs of victims and vulnerable people first." He should get an award for something or other.

A tax return returned by HMRC

Back in 2013, HMRC accused a man from Evesham of failing to answer one of the questions on his tax return correctly. To the question "Do you have anyone dependent on you?" he responded: "2.1 million illegal immigrants, 1.1 million crackheads, 4.4 million unemployable Jeremy Kyle scroungers, 900,000 criminals in over 85 prisons, plus 650 idiots in parliament, and the whole of the European Commission."

When HMRC told him the response was unacceptable, he asked: "Who did I miss out?"

Proceeding at a great rate – a floor in the system

A Supreme Court ruling in 2017 gave the Valuation Office Agency – an executive agency of HMRC – the right to levy business rates individually on offices on separate floors and corridors where they had previously been treated as single premises. If firms occupy an entire building, that's one premises; but if you operate from different parts of a building alongside parts occupied by others, each section is rated separately. The VOA justified this ridiculous decision – which proved highly expensive for up to 30,000 businesses (mainly small ones) – by saying: "The agency has a responsibility to maintain a correct and up-to-date rating list. As a result of the Supreme Court's decision, we had to change how we value some properties for business rates." Had to. Of course.

How big is that again?

A *Sky News* reporter once informed us, on several occasions, that a national park in the Democratic Republic of Congo was "three times the size of Luxembourg". Any ideas on how big that might be?

Variations on a theme

- "Well, it may be all right in practice, but it will never work in theory." – Warren Buffett on how the academic community regarded his investment approach.
- "An economist is someone who says, when an idea works in practice, 'let's see if it works in theory.'" – Walter W. Heller, chairman of the Council of Economic Advisers in President John F. Kennedy's administration in the early 1960s.

- "The problem with QE (quantitative easing) is that it works in practice, but it doesn't work in theory." – Ben Bernanke, chairman of the US Federal Reserve, in 1914.
- "In theory there is no difference between theory and practice. In practice there is." – Lawrence Peter "Yogi" Berra, an American professional baseball catcher who became a manager and coach.
- "This may work very well in practice, Minister, but it doesn't work in theory." – supposed comment by a Whitehall mandarin to his Secretary of State.
- "In theory, theory and practice are the same. In practice, they are not." – Albert Einstein.
- "In theory there is very little difference between theory and practice; in practice there's a hell of a lot of difference." – John Mariotti, president and CEO of The Enterprise Group.

Accessibility: no loos is the choice

In 2004, a couple in Kent applied to Shepway council to install a lavatory at the back of a small storeroom for the use of tenants (refugees from Zimbabwe). Planning officials insisted that it be accessible to wheelchairs – at considerable extra cost. The couple pointed out that the door to the storeroom was not wide enough for a wheelchair and that it would be impossible for any wheelchair user to reach the lavatory anyway but the officials (what a great word) said this did not concern them: they were complying with the law. This decision came at the same time as Shepway council was closing down all the public lavatories in Folkestone, largely because of the excessive cost of converting them to allow wheelchair access.

Toughening up on identity checks

In November 2016 the writer and broadcaster Vivienne Parry, who lived in north London, wrote to *The Times* to say: "Recently I was asked to show a photo ID before I could register with a London GP practice. I showed my National Union of Journalists press card. It was roundly rejected. Identification that would get me through to the front line in a war zone is apparently not enough to get me into the NHS in Camden."

Awards for "nonsense" and "gibberish"

Back in 2012, the Plain English Campaign handed out "Golden Bull" awards for the "worst written nonsense". Right up there was this explanation from NHS North Staffordshire of why it had rejected an application for a new pharmacy at a doctor's surgery. "There was not currently a gap on the spectrum of adequacy sufficient to conclude that the provision of pharmaceutical services is not currently secured to the standard of adequacy." It also presented a "Foot in Mouth" Award, for spoken gibberish, to Mitt Romney, the defeated US presidential candidate. He had told voters: "I believe in an America where millions of Americans believe in an America that's the America millions of Americans believe in. That's the America I love." And so do we all.

- In 2004 the Plain English Campaign, which has members in 70 countries, asked 5,000 of its members to come up with a list of the 10 most irritating or hackneyed expressions. "At the end of the day" was a clear winner, followed by "at this moment in time". Third, curiously, was "like" as, like, a form of punctuation. Then came: "with all due respect"; "to be honest"; "let's touch base"; "I hear what you're saying"; "going forward"; "absolutely"; and "blue sky thinking". Just missing out on the top 10 were "between a rock and a hard place" and "it's not rocket science". As one correspondent wrote at the time, "At the end of the day, there was basically no competition." Perhaps most surprisingly, that staple of football analysts and politicians, "I have to say", didn't gain a top ranking. To be honest, and with all due respect, at the end of the day, it should absolutely have been up there with the best of them.

Getting the views of the average taxi driver...

Some years back the BBC *News 24* programme announced an interview with the editor of "Newswireless", a technology website, on the subject of a court case involving Apple computers but ended up inadvertently speaking to a taxi driver who had been waiting for a client in the foyer of the BBC. Interestingly, the editor of the website was able to watch the interview on a large screen in the foyer. Asked if he was surprised by the verdict in the case, the taxi driver responded: "I am very surprised to see ... this verdict to come on me because I was not expecting that. When I came they told me something else and I am coming. So a big surprise anyway." The interviewer pressed on:

"With regards to the costs involved, do you think more people will now be downloading online?" and received the reply: "Actually if you can walk everywhere you are going to see a lot of people downloading the internet and the website and everything they want. But I think it is much better for development and to inform people what they want and to get the easy way and so faster if they are looking for." You really can't say fairer than that and full marks to the cab driver for an explanation of which any politician – and maybe the real editor – would have been proud.

An interesting way of treating visitors

The author used to lead groups of tourists on sightseeing tours in Africa and elsewhere. Landing on one occasion at Arusha airport in Tanzania, I was watching the members of the group proceed through immigration when a soldier approached and asked if I was carrying much money. "No," I said, "this is largely a pre-paid expedition and we only need some small amounts of spending money." The soldier retreated but as the last of the party had his passport stamped, an immigration officer took me aside and asked me to accompany him into a side room. He introduced me to someone else there for no apparent reason – we shook hands – and then the immigration official sat at a desk and began to thumb through a book. I enquired gently if there was a problem and he responded that there was indeed a problem – with my papers. That seemed a little odd as no one had looked at them yet and they consisted of no more than a British passport with a visa for the country. He continued thumbing and after a while said, without looking up, "We are trying to help you. Have you brought us a gift?" Given the choice of spending a lengthy spell in this office while the tour party waited in the heat aboard our coach, or handing over a bottle of duty-free whisky so we could be reunited, I chose the latter and this solved the problem completely, apart from one last question: "Are you giving us this of your own free will?" What could I say but "Of course!"? My passport was then stamped and an amazing tour got under way.

Service with a smile ... and a brilliant excuse

The wayside café in Gloucestershire looked inviting and we were hungry so we pulled in. "Would you like something to drink?" asked the waitress cheerfully. "I'd like an orange juice with lemonade," I replied. "Do you want two drinks?" she enquired. "No. Just orange juice with lemonade." "You want them in the same glass?" "Yes please." "I don't think we can do that," she said – and they didn't. I received a glass of each. When it came to food, my son opted for the grill. "Would you like chicken or lamb?" Miss Cheerful asked. "I'll have the chicken," said son. Some minutes later the waitress returned and said, "Sorry, but the man who cooks the chicken hasn't come in today." "That's OK," said son, a little bemused, "I'll have the lamb." To which the waitress responded, "We haven't got any lamb." We haven't returned to that café but someday we really must.

Women's rights ... a long-running issue

"While Europe's eye is fix'd on mighty things,
The fate of empires and the fall of kings;
While quacks of State must each produce his plan,
And even children lisp the Rights of Man;
Amid this mighty fuss just let me mention,
The Rights of Woman merit some attention."

      –   Robert (Rabbie) Burns (1759-1796)

              –

Just how wrong can anyone be?

In 1947, the founder of IBM, one Thomas J. Watson announced: "I think there is a world market for about five computers." And in 1977, Ken Olson, president of a business called Digital Equipment Corporation, stated: "There is no reason for any individual to have a computer in their home."

Last words

And finally...

The UK remains, of course, one of the world's best countries in which to live and the scramble by immigrants to get in attests to its reputation.

This four-nation country, with various islands added on, contains an extraordinary mixture of people and opinions. There are, for example, people who care, passionately, about the colour of clothing worn by television newsreaders when announcing the death of a royal personage (especially ties for male presenters), which to some might seem dotty; and we have members of the royal family, including the monarch and her eldest son, who believe in the curative powers of homoeopathy, the brainchild of a German doctor in the late 18th century, which, in its purest form, amounts to taking in water – a little if you are feeling only slightly off colour and more if symptoms persist. This support for homoeopathy, likened by the BMA to witchcraft, provoked one columnist in *The Times* to write (in 2013) that "loyalty to the Crown shouldn't require deference to drivel".

Eccentricity – mostly harmless – is all around us. The Department of Transport hands a major contract for HS2 to a company that is known to be a basket-case heading into the arms of the liquidators and not many months later hands a shipping contract to a company with no ships – both acts of charming barminess but also horribly expensive. Nincompoopery of the highest order!

It's a country, and not the only one, where footballers can earn in a week what many people take 10 years to achieve and in a year considerably more than most people can earn in a lifetime of hard labour. If someone appears on TV or in a film, then newspapers and even broadcasters will instantly describe that person as a celebrity. And should such person appear in what is known as a "reality" programme – which is generally as far from reality as one could hope to get – then fame is virtually guaranteed.

Actors and singers frequently carry more weight than politicians in campaigning for changes in society, whether they are urging us less well-known mortals to part with our money to help people or animals in need in the UK or in lands far away, or asking us to eat less meat (or none at all), use less plastic, cut down on travel by car or plane, etc., etc.

In 2012, reforms to the National Health Service which were designed to cut bureaucracy resulted in a substantial increase in the numbers of bureaucrats.

Meanwhile, reforms to the probation service resulted in chaos and measures designed to save money cost vastly more than they saved; and an efficiency drive in Whitehall, which started in 2013 and was expected to make savings of £128 million a year, actually cost far more than it saved.

That same year, the public accounts committee of the House of Commons reported that taxpayers were losing £55 billion a year because of fraud, error and unpaid taxes and described, with typical British understatement, the scale of the losses as "worryingly high". At the same time, the National Fraud Authority said it estimated the true cost of fraud to the public sector in Britain was £20.6 billion a year.

There is not enough money to keep libraries or day-care centres open or repair potholes but plenty for projects such as HS2 and other crazy and crazily expensive schemes – such as a new bridge across the Thames which cost well over £60 million in preparatory charges but will never be built.

It's topsy-turvy – but who would want to change it? Apart from almost everyone.

Acknowledgements

• The UK's national newspapers, including The Times and Sunday Times, The Daily Telegraph and The Sunday Telegraph, The Guardian, The Observer, Daily Mail, The Sun, Daily Express, Daily Star, The Independent, the i, Financial Times, etc.; plus a considerable number of regional and local newspapers, including some published outside the UK, too many to mention.

• Websites of the government, regulators and other bodies in the UK (roughly in order of appearance):

UK Government	www.gov.uk
Office of Water Service	www.ofwat.gov.uk
Water Industry Commission for Scotland	www.watercommission.co.uk
Utility Regulator (Northern Ireland)	www.uregni.gov.uk
Consumer Council for Water	www.ccwater.org.uk
Drinking Water Inspectorate	www.dwi.gov.uk
Office of Gas and Electricity Markets	www.ofgem.gov.uk
Office of Communications	www.ofcom.org.uk
Office of Road and Rail	https://orr.gov.uk
Network Rail	www.networkrail.co.uk
World Economic Forum: Global Competitiveness Reports	www.weforum.org
Health and Safety Executive	www.hse.gov.uk
Health and Safety Executive Northern Ireland	www.hseni.gov.uk
Environment Agency	www.gov.uk/government/organisations/environment-agency
Natural Resources Wales	https://naturalresources.wales
Scottish Environment Protection Agency	www.sepa.org.uk
Northern Ireland Environment Agency	www.daera-ni.gov.uk/northern-ireland-environment-agency
Information Commissioner's Office	https://ico.org.uk
Surveillance Camera Commissioner	www.gov.uk/government/organisations/surveillance-camera-commissioner
Gambling Commission	www.gamblingcommission.gov.uk
[Senet group (promoting "responsible gambling standards")]	[https://senetgroup.org.uk]
Competition and Markets Authority	www.gov.uk/government/organisations/competition-and-markets-authority
UK Competition Network	www.gov.uk/government/groups/uk-competition-network
National Trading Standards	www.nationaltradingstandards.uk
Northern Ireland Trading Standards Service	www.nidirect.gov.uk
Trading Standards Scotland	www.tsscot.co.uk
Chartered Trading Standards Institute	www.facebook.com/CharteredTradingStandardsInstitute
Charity Commission	www.gov.uk/government/organisations/charity-commission
Scottish Charity Regulator	www.oscr.org.uk

The Charity Commission for Northern Ireland	www.charitycommissionni.org.uk
Electoral Commission	www.electoralcommission.org.uk
Care Quality Commission	https://cqc.org.uk
Healthcare Inspectorate Wales	https://hiw.org.uk
Healthcare Improvement Scotland	www.healthcareimprovementscotland.org
Regulation and Quality Improvement Authority (Northern Ireland)	https://rqia.org.uk
NHS Improvement	https://improvement.nhs.uk
Civil Aviation Authority	www.caa.co.uk
Transport Focus	www.transportfocus.org.uk
Office for Nuclear Regulation	www.onr.org.uk
Single Source Regulations Office (Ministry of Defence)	www.gov.uk/government/organisations/single-source-regulations-office
Groceries Code Adjudicator	www.gov.uk/government/organisations/groceries-code-adjudicator
Forensic Science Regulator	www.gov.uk/government/organisations/forensic-science-regulator
The UK Regulators Network	www.ukrn.org.uk
Regulators' Code	www.gov.uk/government/publications/regulators-code
Bank of England	www.bankofengland.co.uk
Office for National Statistics	www.ons.gov.uk
Financial Conduct Authority	www.fca.org.uk
Office for Professional Body Anti-Money Laundering	www.fca.org.uk/opbas
National Audit Office	www.nao.org.uk
Independent Parliamentary Standards Authority	www.theipsa.org.uk
The Pensions Regulator	www.thepensionsregulator.gov.uk
Advertising Standards Authority	www.asa.org.uk
The British Broadcasting Corporation (BBC)	www.bbc.com
Independent Press Standards Organisation (IPSO)	www.ipso.co.uk
The Independent Monitor for the Press (Impress)	https://impress.press
Regulator of Community Interest Companies	www.gov.uk/government/organisations/office-of-the-regulator-of-community-interest-companies
Leveson Inquiry (2012)	www.gov.uk/government/publications/leveson-inquiry-report-into-the-culture-practices-and-ethics-of-the-press
Press Recognition Panel (PRP)	www.pressrecognitionpanel.org.uk
Index on Censorship	www.indexoncensorship.org
Committees of Advertising Practice	www.cap.org.uk
Criminal Cases Review Commission	https://ccrc.gov.uk
The Crown Prosecution Service	www.cps.gov.uk
Equality and Human Rights Commission	www.equalityhumanrights.com
The Monitoring Group	www.tmg-uk.org
National Centre for Social Research	www.natcen.ac.uk
College of Policing	www.college.police.uk
Campaign Against Antisemitism	https://antisemitism.uk
The Crown Estate	www.thecrownestate.co.uk
Duchy of Lancaster	www.duchyoflancaster.co.uk
Duchy of Cornwall	https://duchyofcornwall.org

Privy Council	https://privycouncil.independent.gov.uk
Privy Council Office	www.gov.uk/government/organisations/privy-council-office
Judicial Committee of the Privy Council	www.jcpc.uk/
International Development Committee (UK Parliament)	www.parliament.uk/.../commons-select/international-development-committee
Independent Commission for Aid Impact	https://icai.independent.gov.uk
Plain English Campaign	https://plainenglish.co.uk

• Other websites:

Reporters Without Borders	https://rsf.org/en
Hacked Off	https://hackinginquiry.org
Transparency International	www.transparency.org
Encyclopaedia Britannica	www.britannica.com
World Health Organization	www.who.int
United Nations Children's Fund (UNICEF)	www.unicef.org
National Geographic	www.nationalgeographic.com
Human Rights Watch	www.hrw.org
Freedom House	www.freedomhouse.org
Water Charity for Safe Water and Sanitation	www.water.org
Oxfam	www.oxfam.org.uk
Save the Children Fund	www.savethechildren.org.uk
World Bank Group	www.worldbank.org

The Author

The author drifted into journalism when he edited the student newspaper at the University of Canterbury in New Zealand for two years in the early 1960s – where he was studying to become a secondary school teacher. Subsequently, while turning his attention to economics and accounting, he was offered jobs on a number of business and agricultural publications. He has lived in Surrey, England, since 1971, making a meagre living editing an assortment of trade and professional publications until his retirement in 2016, since when, as an ageing and slightly cynical writer, he has turned his attention to investigating political machinations and the structure of governmental and regulatory bodies in the UK and elsewhere, along with various other aspects of life in general. He has also written a book on Christianity – how it is and how it was meant to be, which is available on Amazon Kindle under the title Simply Wonderful, Wonderfully Simple.

See other GBP titles

(Scan with a smart or iPad phone and click on the text that come up)

www.gbpublishing.co.uk/lifestyle